If Wishes Were Horses

If Wishes Were Horses

by John Perrotta

Author's note:

Certain historical facts and actual names contained within
should be considered to exist within the context of the
fiction portrayed around them. The fictional characters are
not intended to resemble any person, living or dead and any
similarity is coincidental.

First Edition.
Cover design by Jen Ferguson

ISBN: 978-1514384862

For Gina, Liza, Tony and Aidan

The truth knocks on the door and you say, "Go away, I'm looking for the truth," and so it goes away.

-- Zen and the Art of Motorcycle Maintenance

PART I

CHAPTER 1

The corner of Broadway and Caroline Street in Saratoga is just about the center of town, the spot where you can see most everything there is to see. And in early August of 1972 when the races were running, the town was filled with carloads of tourists either down from the shores of Lake George or up from the stifling city, taking a couple of weeks respite as they camped out in the Adirondacks on inflatable mattresses in pop-up tents or little log cabins.

And those day-trippers hoping to spot a top class race horse over at the track on Union Avenue, maybe a Kentucky Derby prospect for next year, so they could say they had a couple of bucks on him when they saw him break his maiden.

From where Hamilton Greer stood on that corner, he could see everyone and their uncle in both directions, some ready to picnic at the races, lugging those huge wicker baskets full of sandwiches and deviled eggs and soda pop, and of course, cake.

And as a smart man once observed, "cake is what holds a family together." But Hamilton hadn't had cake for a long time...

He was just as happy to leave that family behind, his mom and a new step-dad who badgered him to cut his hair and go out for a team, any team, or go get a job at the ski resort and bring home some money. He'd turned sixteen the day before when he stuffed his duffel bag with an extra pair of jeans and a couple of tee-shirts and a sweater, went down to the bus station and bought a ticket on the first Greyhound going wherever he could get to for twelve bucks, hoping he might find gainful employment before he went through the rest of the cash he'd squirreled away.

Hamilton Greer took it all in, barely awake after what felt like a long night sleeping on the hard slats of a wooden bench in Congress Park next to the Canfield Casino, a place where the guy on the bus said Diamond Jim Brady and Bet a Million Gates used to gamble all night before the city fathers decided to make such behavior illegal. Now, he said, they just use the gambling hall for parties and nobody ever bothers you in that park.

A kid passing with an armful of newspapers looked about his age.

"You selling those?" said Hamilton.

"Nah," said the kid, "Tellies for my old man and his pals, so they can pick another bunch of losers to throw their money away on."

Hamilton wasn't sure what that meant.

"Tellies?"

"*Morning Telegraph*, the racing paper. So they can handicap the horses."

Hamilton nodded, trying to act like he <u>didn't</u> think the kid was speaking Greek.

"You a runaway?" said the kid.

Hamilton just shrugged but the kid knew he was right.

"Looking for a job," said Hamilton.

"There's always work over at the track," said the kid, "Get there first thing at dawn, the stable gate on Union Avenue, you can get a job walking hots."

Which drew another blank from Hamilton. He didn't want to but he asked anyway:

"What're hots?"

"Horses, stupid, the ones that gallop around the track and come back hot and sweaty. Sheesh."

Then the kid smiled just so Hamilton wouldn't feel too foolish.

"Thanks," said Hamilton.

"Good luck," said the kid.

Hamilton glanced at the pocket watch his old man had given him before he split, a silver Elgin, telling him it had belonged to his grandfather. Dawn was barely breaking and the watch read a quarter past five when he stashed his duffel bag behind a marble statue of a naked Greek or Roman woman and headed up the hill to Union Avenue to look for the stable gate for "Oklahoma," which is the name they call the training area across the street from the main track.

He was sitting on a bench with a rag-tag bunch of hopefuls by that gate when a shiny Cadillac sedan rolled up.

"You, c'mon," said the trainer, motioning to him to hop in the front seat and two other guys to get in the back.

"Anybody walked hots before?"

Silence until the half-a-hipster looking kid wearing a black hasty-brim cracked:

"Just hold on and keep turning left."

"And don't let go whatever you do," laughed the trainer.

Hamilton watched the other guys grab the long leather shanks from the grooms as they led their horses inside the barn, into the shedrow, one after another as the riders dismounted and went to dunk their bridles in a bucket of water. He figured he'd do what the other guys do, and like the hipster said, keep turning left.

"Thirty minutes," said the groom, pointing to a clock on the wall, handing Hamilton a shank connected to the biggest animal he'd ever been that close to.

"Don't worry, he's only half-fit and pretty tired, won't give you no trouble," said the groom.

"Just keep turning left," said Hamilton and the groom smiled.

The newness of the rest of that first day flew by for him, walking half-a-dozen horses and holding them while they got a bath, but Hamilton felt like he'd passed some rite of passage when one of the horses reared up and looked for sure like it was going to take off, but he hung on, giving the horse some slack and a chance to calm down and he got a nod of approval from one of the grooms.

He finished hosing off the asphalt and raking the shedrow before he realized that everyone had disappeared, most off to the track kitchen for some lunch or the others that went to sack out in the tack rooms where they lived. The foreman told him there'd be a regular job and a cot for him if he wanted to stick around.

"Highly skilled labor," he kidded.

Hamilton retrieved his duffel bag from the park and stopped at Sadie's Chicken Shack, considering that he was a working man now and it might be okay to splurge for a couple of bucks, filling his belly with fried chicken and sweet potatoes before he went back to what could be his new home.

And the western sky got black like it does often in that part of the country late in the afternoon as a chill gust began to blow through the damp summer heat to signal that an Adirondack thunder storm was about to hit, so Hamilton hustled to get back to the barn and sure enough just when he did, a gully-washer tore through.

The rumbling thunder and forks of lightning were so close they rattled the barns as a hot wind blew the bandages and saddlecloths off the clotheslines where they'd been hung out to dry. The grooms made haste to dig a channel so the water wouldn't run inside the shedrow, and instead when it poured down hard for ten minutes straight the puddles connected to make a huge lake in the space between that barn and the next, covering the walking ring where Hamilton had guided a few hots that morning.

Then the sun appeared in the western sky and the air was cool.

The next couple of days Hamilton got bit or stepped on a half a dozen times but counted himself lucky that he never got kicked while he was learning which side of the horses to walk on which everybody called the 'right' side but was really the left.

Only one of the other hotwalkers that came on board when Hamilton did was still around, a kid they called

Spider, who looked short enough to be a jockey. That wasn't the name he came with but he stepped lightly on his feet with a quick little strut and that was the racetrack name one of the grooms hung on him the first day.

They slept in the same tack room the first week and Hamilton was thinking that Spider might be a runaway too since he had little more than the clothes on his back with him and he figured they might have a lot in common.

But Spider was downright evasive when Hamilton tried to engage him in conversation and he usually wouldn't give an answer, nor even look him in the eye if he did.

"Have any brothers or sisters?" Hamilton asked.

"I'm one of a kind," said Spider.

"Where 'you from?" said Hamilton.

"All over," said Spider, volunteering nothing.

Hamilton didn't take it personally since Spider behaved pretty much that same way with everyone and that was how Spider got by.

He'd only been at Barn 43 for a couple of weeks, but Hamilton finally felt settled in, comfortable with his surroundings when the trainer gave him a place to stay in a tack room, sharing the space with Willie, one of the grooms. Willie looked like he might be old enough to be a grandpa and said he'd been on the track for fifty years.

Hamilton thought that was better than bunking with Spider, who had already started to get on his nerves.

Some folks found Willie a little cranky, but he took to Hamilton right away, christening him with a racetrack name, "Ham and Eggs," or just "Ham" and pretty soon everybody around the barn was calling him one or the other.

He had a sense that life there might be different from back home, where everybody wanted him to act the way they wanted. Here they left him alone if he did his job and they all seemed to have a genuine interest in what he had to say. Ham had only just finished his junior year with good grades and thought he was the smart one around there until one day Jake the shedrow foreman told him he was from Vermont too, and had a degree in political science from UVM. He had white hair and wore those wire-rimmed glasses and did sort of look like a teacher.

When Lizzie the exercise girl from England let it slip that she'd given up a career in accounting to be near the horses, she said it was "because horses don't let you down like people do." Lizzie was blonde and pretty and Ham didn't know why but he usually felt extra shy around her so he let her do most of the talking.

And even Carlos the groom, who had a family back in South America and sent all his money home, had a university degree but said he too thought it was a better life here, working outdoors and taking care of beautiful animals instead of cooped up inside like he was before, a clerk in a government office.

So it was in a way a lot like a family there in the Evans stable where they treated Hamilton like the kid brother, pulling pranks on him for being the rookie, when they sent him to the furthest barn in the stable area to ask old lady Madigan for a bucket of steam and her yelling at him to get the hell out of there or she'd give him a bucket of something all over his dumb ass.

Or when Jake told him they were going to work the big mare and to hurry up and go get the key to the quarter pole and he fell for that one too.

Willie hailed from Kentucky where he'd grown up around horses and he seemed content with his life at the track, rarely leaving the barn area except maybe once or twice a week when he went to the grocery store after some canned soup to heat up on his hot-plate in the tack room for those times when he didn't feel like going to the track kitchen.

Unless of course, one of his horses was running, when he'd put on his game face and the best shirt he could find, start brushing and polishing that horse until its butt shined like a mirror with not a speck of dust on it.

He was a tall man, the only one in the barn taller than Ham and had big, strong hands and meaty forearms and always dressed in khaki work clothes and a straw hat and on his face he wore a permanent look of concern, thick grey eyebrows furrowed over those dark eyes.

It was Willie who took Ham over to the security office to get his racetrack license, and luckily he had gotten himself a driver's permit before he left Vermont, even though he never got to drive, but it did prove he was over sixteen and that's the minimum age to work on the track.

Ham could tell Willie enjoyed having a pupil, someone to whom he could pass on his years of experience. He taught him how to use a hoof-pick to clean the horses' feet and how to roll the standing bandages so they'd go on even and how to comb the straw out of their tails and how to rub them shiny with a rag and how to give them a bath and a hundred other things, but most importantly, how to keep them happy.

And he realized that Willie was one of those people who felt more comfortable around animals than he did around other people, almost like he was tuned in on the horses' wavelength and didn't really care about the people, maybe accounting for what some thought was a slightly standoffish manner. But he always took the time to answer whenever Ham had a question, and occasionally Willie would digress with a tale from his own life and before Ham realized it their conversations had turned into a lesson.

He knew his roommate was the best groom in the barn but before long Ham began to wonder if Willie could read or write. He wasn't sure but he considered how to deal with that if it were truly the case. He didn't want to embarrass him, but he did want to help Willie if Willie wanted help.

He guessed that somehow the old man had figured out on his own how to understand the past performance charts in the racing paper, but those were mostly numbers and he for sure couldn't read the articles with that magnifying glass.

And Ham began to look forward to when they would take a horse over to run in a race. He'd carry the bucket with a sponge and a brush and a girth channel and a rub-rag in it and walk alongside as the old man led his pride across Union Avenue to the open area among those tall oak trees that each had a number nailed to them.

Ham had never been to a horse race before, but Willie told him Saratoga was the only track where they let the trainers saddle their horses under a tree and not in a fenced-in paddock. It did seem odd that fans could walk right up to the horses and sure enough, once in a while a frisky colt or filly would rear up and scatter everyone and some folks would say they need to put a rail around here so nobody gets hurt and some others would say nah, leave it like it is.

It was the middle of a sunny Wednesday afternoon and Ham was raking the shedrow in a neat kris-cross pattern the way Mister Evans liked it, and he realized that he liked it too, keeping the barn neat like a showplace, with potted plants hanging from the awnings and the stone jockey painted in the red and yellow stable colors outside standing sentinel.

Ham's job that day included holding the horses for the blacksmith and he'd just finished shoeing a couple when Willie whistled and motioned to Ham to come along.

"Gonna' see yourself something special today, boy," said Willie.

The horses were already saddled and the jockeys just getting a leg up when Ham and Willie got there. From fifty yards away though, above the heads of the crowd they could see the copper shine of the big chestnut colt topped with his rider in the blue and white block silks.

"Secretariat," said Willie.

"Wow," said Ham.

"He'll win as far as you can throw a rock," said Willie as Ham followed him to the betting windows.

"You ever make a wager, son?" said Willie.

"Uh-uh," said Ham.

They got in the queue and Ham took out two bucks. He'd had a few paychecks, been starting to save some money and he couldn't see how much Willie was going to bet, but they were in a line marked "$2 WPS."

"Tell the man, 'two dollars to win on number two,'" said Willie, "last time you ever going to see that horse <u>not</u> be favorite."

"Okay," said Ham, but when he got to the window he was nervous and just held out his two dollars and told the ticket seller "Secretariat," but the man knew what he meant and punched out a yellow win ticket with a black number two on it.

The announcer's call echoed through the stands and across the track they could see the other horses rush away from the gate, Secretariat's silks back in last. After about a quarter-mile though, the big chestnut began to pick up speed and cruised around the others to draw off in the end, winning by five easy lengths.

They crowded near the fence to watch a tall blonde lady and a little white-haired man, waiting by the chalk circle on the track where the winning horse would stand to have his picture taken.

"Best horse 'since Man o' War," said Willie, "You'll see."

Before they went back to the barn, they stopped at the cashier's window to collect their winnings and Ham was happy to get five bucks back for the two he'd bet, but he realized there sure was a lot of money flying around the place. He peeked back and watched as Willie scooped a pile of twenties off the counter and stuffed them in his pocket.

Ten days later, they made a point of getting to the frontside early so they could see Secretariat's trainer put on the saddle and have a few words with his jockey before he tossed him up, way up there on the big colt's back. They were so close they could hear the men talk but they were speaking French and neither Ham nor Willie could understand a word they said.

Willie was moving faster than usual and Ham had to hustle to keep up as they climbed the stairs to the second floor, passing right by the ticket sellers.

"We have to bet, don't we?" said Ham.

"Listen 'what I say, boy," said Willie, pointing to the odds board, "Ain't a horse alive worth two-to-five, not even this one. He should win for fun, but we 'just here to watch and enjoy it today."

And watch they did, from a perfect spot at the top of the grandstand where one of Willie's friends was an usher. Secretariat took his time again, strolling out of the gate last and charging past the other horses like they weren't there and the crowd roared, knowing they were seeing history in the making.

"See, we should have bet," said Ham.

"Costs too much for what you do get, if you don't get nothing when you're wrong," said Willie, "Just be glad to see a good horse run, boy, 'there's gonna be plenty 'times to bet when you get the right odds."

Willie always carried a soft woven cloth in his back pocket, called it his 'rub-rag' and that's what he used it for, to rub on his three horses until they shined and shined... and shined.

The grey mare was named Delilah and she was big and good-looking and good-natured, even playful and she'd switch her tail and shake all over, quivering when Willie rubbed on her. He'd sing to her like Tom Jones when he gave her a bath:

"*My--my--my-- De-li-lah...*" and he'd laugh and laugh.

They only took her across the road to run that one time and she broke slow and closed some ground in the stretch to finish third and wasn't ever much of a threat to the winner, but Willie seemed happy enough and he said the turns were too tight for her there but she'd win one for sure when they got back down to "Big Sandy" which was what he called Belmont Park. He said some trainers liked to train their horses into shape and some liked to race them into shape and Evans was one of the latter.

Willie said that old hard-knocking bay gelding Momma's Boy was his "bread and butter" horse because although he only ran in cheap claiming races, even if he didn't win he still always seemed to hit the board and that got Willie extra commission money, what they called "barn-stakes." He had run two seconds and a third in the past month, did his job well and even though Willie didn't have a win at Saratoga, those 'extras' added up.

The other horse Willie took care of was a two year old called Mighty who had a stripe of white trickling down the front of his handsome bay face and he was just a baby compared to the others, but he was named right, big and strong and full of youthful energy. Willie said he thought Mighty could be any kind, maybe even a stakes horse, but no doubt he'd be ready for a maiden race soon and he thought if Mister Evans let him run with blinkers on, they'd be betting their money and he'd win the first time out.

Ham liked how the horses all had different personalities and he liked how Willie treated them, as if they were kids on a team he was coaching. And how he talked to them like they were kids, gentle and never cross or mean, but firm and serious when they needed it, kind and playful when they needed that too.

By the last weekend of the Saratoga race meet Ham was feeling restless.

"Where to next?" he asked Willie.

"New York, New York..." said Willie, "...so big they had to name it twice."

The track finished up on a Sunday and the following morning the horse vans lined up like a great caravan, queuing to use the loading ramps as the barn area emptied out. Most of the stables were heading to Belmont and some to Aqueduct and a few to Jersey or Kentucky and soon the training area would be deserted. The whole crew would be moving on except Spider, who'd gone missing, but everyone just assumed he'd hit the road again, since on the racetrack people came and went all the time.

Ham lugged the duffel bag with his possessions and tossed it in the bay of the van he would ride with Willie and his three horses from their stable as well as half a dozen from another barn. The groom with the other horses was a kid he knew named Miguel who had a thin moustache and looked older but probably wasn't more than eighteen. He spent most of the ride fussing over a big bay colt and when Ham started talking about Secretariat, he scoffed.

"My champion," said Miguel, "beats that big red horse next time."

"No way," said Ham.

"Five bucks he does," said Miguel.

"What's his name?" said Ham, shaking his hand and taking the bet.

"Stop the Music," said Miguel.

CHAPTER 2

A caravan of horse trailers rolled down the Hudson River Valley past Albany as the slightest touch of color on the mountainsides hinted at the coming change of season.

All the horses behaved well on the ride to Belmont, allowing Ham to enjoy most of the trip with his head poked out an open side window, feeling the warm Indian Summer breeze. It was the furthest south Hamilton Greer had ever been.

He'd see a guy zip past in a fancy set of wheels, maybe a Cadillac sedan or a Lincoln convertible with the top down, and the guy would glance up and they'd make eye contact for a second and Ham would imagine that could be him and wondered what it must be like, driving home to your wife and kids in your big house and maybe some of the horses on that van belonged to him.

After about four hours their van crossed the Hudson on the upper level of the George Washington bridge and Ham could see the tops of the Empire State building and the Chrysler building with their tapered tops and steel spires. They passed through an area redolent of an immense city, with stores and apartment houses and highrise buildings everywhere you looked, until they crossed another bridge and it got greener. The driver made the sweeping turn off the Cross Island Parkway onto Hempstead Turnpike and as they rolled up to the stable gate, Willie said:

"Home, sweet home..."

Belmont Park itself was even more grand than Ham had imagined from Willie's description, with a track considerably wider than the one at Saratoga and a mile and a half around instead of a mile and an eighth and inside that, not just one verdant turf course but two.

And if it wasn't as quaint outside the gates as Saratoga, it seemed even more pastoral inside the stable area, with plenty of huge oak trees and no shortage of grassy space on which to graze the horses.

When they arrived the stalls were all bedded with fresh straw and the water buckets were filled and the webbings clean and shiny, so all they had to do was walk the horses right in and hang their hay-nets. Outside the trainer's office, a stone jockey just like the one at Saratoga stood guard, surrounded by red and yellow marigolds.

Ham and Willie had a larger tack room to live in and everything about the stable was a lot bigger than before, since it now included so many of the Evans' horses that didn't make the trip upstate, the ones that had stayed there at Belmont for the past two months.

Their work routine stayed pretty much the same as it was at Saratoga, early morning training and quiet afternoons after the vets and the blacksmith left, and although Ham found it easy enough to make friends among the racetrackers, most days he preferred to hang around with Willie, enjoying the secure world inside the stable gates. The other stable workers got used to seeing them together, engaged in what seemed like endless conversations, the kid concentrating in rapt attention like a Greek scholar at the foot of his mentor.

In the evening after supper they'd walk over to the basketball court and if the younger guys were there, Ham would play and Willie would watch or if they weren't there, the two of them would shoot some H-O-R-S-E until it got too dark to see.

"Boss man 'be here Saturday," said Willie, "'Axed me 'was you up to rubbing some. What y'all think?"

His "think" sounded like "thank," which Ham got a kick out of, never having been around Southern accents before, so unlike the clipped New England twang with the long 'a' he was used to.

"'Think I'm as ready as I'll ever be," said Ham.

"He said you can take the two next to me, those maidens and look after Chester too," said Willie, "Pay's a buck and a quarter."

Chester was the stable pony and ponies don't win any purses or get any extra stake money, but Ham saw it as part of the deal starting out, that he'd more than double his check from sixty a week and besides, he was moving up the ladder.

Next morning Ham was up and dressed before his alarm clock had a chance to go off. He hustled down the shedrow to his horses and found Chester and the black mare Starlight waiting at the front of their stalls, but the bay gelding Buckeye had parked himself in the middle of his with his right front foot pointed out wide, not putting any weight on it.

"Shoot," said Ham, and he went to look for Willie right away, not sure how serious that might be but figuring Willie would know for sure if it was.

Willie was in the stall with Delilah, down on one knee in the straw with his back to Ham as he took off her night bandages, running his hands over her knees and ankles and feet to check for any heat.

"Buckeye's lame," said Ham.

"Pointing that right front like a hunting dog on a covey of quail," said Willie, not even looking up.

"Yeah, how'd you know?"

"He cost two hundred thousand but he got a chip 'took out and come here with that right ankle," said Willie, "Arth-a-ritis."

Willie showed Ham how to put the horse in a tub of ice up to his knees and afterward rub on some liniment and soon Buckeye was moving pretty well. Willie told Ham to make sure Mister Evans' assistant, his daughter Mary, knew that the horse was off, but it wasn't a new thing and she'd probably just have the vet give it a shot of bute. He said getting Buckeye going well enough to run in a race was going to be a challenge to Ham but it wasn't out of reach.

"He's one of them that bad luck is always 'round the corner," said Willie, "As soon as you get 'em going good, better start praying they stay sound."

It was breaking dawn the following day and Ham gave a sigh of relief as he walked down the shedrow to see all three of his charges waiting, heads poked out of their stalls and looking for him.

Buckeye was feeling frisky, bobbing and weaving like a boxer at the front of his stall and as Ham bent to open the foot-box and retrieve a brush the big bay bit him right on his butt, tearing the patch-pocket off his jeans. Willie heard Ham swear in pain and said,

"I 'tole you boy, watch out for that sonofagun, he's only playing but you won't sit right for a week now."

He sent Ham to get some ice from the machine in the feed room, put it in a plastic bag and stuff it down his pants and that bag of ice got to be Ham's best friend for the rest of the day but he suspected Willie was right and it might be a while before he'd get a good night's sleep.

Ham was careful around Buckeye after that but next morning when Liz came back from the track on Starlight, he was paying more attention to her than the horse she was on and the mare stepped square on his foot, not on purpose, but surely painful enough all the same. Around Liz he acted like it was nothing but pretty soon he was as lame as Buckeye had been and hobbled around for the rest of the day and Willie teased him it wasn't often an old man like him walked better than a sixteen-year old kid.

Ham didn't so much appreciate that observation when what he really would have liked was a little sympathy.

"'Nother lesson learned, boy," was all Willie offered, "Sometimes horses are like people, they'll hurt you if you ain't paying attention."

"I hope Chester doesn't feel like he has to keep up with the other two and kick me tomorrow," said Ham.

It came Saturday afternoon and Willie was running Delilah in the last race, so Ham told Toady the hotwalker to take the afternoon off and he'd help Willie, carrying the bucket with the sponge and brush and the girth channel over to the paddock.

An announcement crackled over the stable area P.A. system for the horses in the ninth race to come to the paddock and of course they were ready, Willie always wanting to get there early with Delilah. She was what Willie called a "Saturday" horse, one of those that only ran in allowance races or once in a while in a stakes and he felt it helped her relax if she could walk around the ring a few times and have herself a good look at the crowd before she got her saddle on.

With Momma's Boy he always waited until the last minute, taking him over in front bandages as to place some doubt in the minds of any trainers who might be thinking about claiming him. That wasn't likely since Momma's Boy had some age on him, and they wouldn't be getting anything special, but Willie loved that old gelding and figured he would take care of him better than anyone else ever could.

Delilah sparkled in the paddock and Mister Evans told them she would easily have been the winner of the beauty contest had it been one, and as Willie handed her and her jockey off to the pony boy, Ham heard him say to the rider:

"See you in the winner's circle, jock."

Ham followed Willie to the grandstand and Willie told him to make himself a "good bet" which he took to mean more than the two-buck stabs he'd made so far, most of them losers when he tried to pick a winner from the

Morning Telegraph. Every time he thought he was getting smart at figuring out which one was best, it seemed like they lost, unless he listened to Willie, who rarely bet on horses from any other barn, and only once in a while from theirs.

"Some horses are betting horses, but most ain't, they just find a way to come up short," he said.

Willie was serious, giving a lesson:

"Better to try and make some good money than to while away your bankroll on favorites. And if you're gonna step up and make a bet on a longshot, make it count. Nobody ever changed anything in their life betting two bucks on a favorite, so when you do love one, don't be afraid to take your shot."

Ham and Willie each went to a different window and Ham had the seller punch out ten tickets for him, five two-dollar wins and five for place, that twenty bucks being his biggest wager ever by far.

The race was nine furlongs, a mile and an eighth, and they watched from the grandstand apron, not far from the finish line, Willie with Delilah's halter and shank looped over his shoulder, Ham still toting that stainless steel bucket.

Delilah took her time at the start, breaking a bit tardy as seemed to be her way of going and she spotted the rest a few lengths into the Clubhouse Turn, but the jockey wasn't bothered with their being last down the backstretch, even when the two leaders opened up half-a-dozen lengths on the field.

As the horses headed around that wide sweeping bend and neared the quarter pole, Delilah still trailed and Ham was about to get concerned when Willie whispered...

"Now she be going, my big mare..."

Ham could see the rider's hands begin to move back and forth as he urged Delilah and she responded right away, first passing one horse, then another and another until finally they straightened for the stretch drive. She was four wide and still a couple of lengths back when they came to the eighth pole but Willie turned and winked at Ham.

"Let's go, son. We 'going to get our picture took," he said.

As the tote board lit up with the prices, so did Ham's eyes. When he saw that Delilah had paid thirty-six dollars to win and eighteen and change to place and did the math in his head, he totaled up how much he would collect and grabbed at his pocket to make sure the tickets were still there, knowing that was more money than he'd ever had.

The winner of every race always has to go to the spit barn for a drug test, so the evening sky was just starting to dim when Willie finished up with Delilah, giving her a bath as Ham held the shank. They'd spent the extra time to graze her on that grassy patch between the barns and Willie kissed the grey mare on her nose and gave her a carrot as he closed the webbing at the front of her stall.

"My girl..." he said and told Ham to come along, we're going out to eat, saying you need celebrate your winners, 'cause in this game you're going to lose a lot more times than you win.

They passed through the stable gate and crossed the Hempstead Turnpike and walked down a couple of blocks to a little Italian place, one of those pizza joints with checkered tablecloths where all the waiters were from Italy and barely spoke English and Willie ordered a glass of red wine for himself and Ham raised his Coke in a toast.

"To Delilah," he said.

"Amen," said Willie.

They feasted on spaghetti and meatballs and garlic bread and finished up with an Italian dessert that Ham had never even heard of before that he said looked like a cream-filled taco and when they were done they were both so full they could hardly move, filled with food and contentment.

"Past my bed-time," said Willie, and Ham laughed, since it was barely half-past-eight and Willie waved a finger and said "no-no-no" as Ham reached in his pocket for some money to pay his part of the check.

"When your horse wins, you can pay," he said.

In the semi-dark of the shedrow Willie stopped about a half-a-dozen paces from their tack room and held up his hand, signaling Ham to wait. He approached the slightly open door slowly, both of them knowing well that they had locked it shut when they left. It was dark inside the room but when he pushed the door open with his foot and reached in to turn on the light they could see right away that they had been robbed.

"Damn," said Willie.

"Oh, man," said Ham.

Ham went straight to his duffel bag, upside down there on his cot with all the contents strewn about. His extra jeans and underwear were still there and his shirts and sweater too but one thing wasn't... his wallet, along with his winning tickets from Delilah nowhere to be seen.

Willie's old leather suitcase was open too, tossed aside, and the bottle of bourbon he took an occasional drink from was gone off the shelf, but he seemed more angered by the insult of intrusion than he was concerned for the loss of his possessions.

"My fault, boy," he said, "Not telling you how to hide your money. You 'got to leave a 'couple dollars laying around to make it easy for them, 'stash the rest where nobody knows." He stood on a chair and reached up into the rafters and pulled down a small packet from its hiding place.

Ham had all he could do to keep from crying, chagrined as he was at being violated in such a way. He clenched his teeth and pursed his lips as he kicked the iron leg of his cot.

"Tough lesson, son, but you'll get more money, and it's only money," said Willie, "Sometimes, if the first thing 'goes bad for you is the worst, then everything after won't seem so hard."

They cleaned the room and when Willie went to the bathroom to wash up Ham buried his face in his pillow and allowed himself a few sobs, vowing he'd never let that happen to him again.

Willie rarely spent the dollar it cost for a *Morning Telegraph* unless he was planning a bet on one of his horses and he wanted to check out the competition. Usually he would split the cost of the paper with another of the grooms or borrow one and keep the information in his head. Ham liked to look for a discarded paper late in the day at the kitchen or the rec hall and he'd bring it back to the tack room to study, figuring that he could compare his picks to the day's results and see how he would have done, had he made any bets.

Willie told him that making picks when he already knew the outcome was called "red-boarding" since the race results were up there for everyone to see in red lights on the tote board after it was all over.

It seemed as if every day there was another story about Secretariat, anticipating his next race in the Futurity at Belmont, all the writers saying how it was going to be hard to find anyone to run against him, let alone one that had a chance to beat him.

One article talked about Miguel's horse, Stop the Music, and although he had already been third to Secretariat at Saratoga, how he was one of the few brave enough to try again and the only one that might have a chance.

"My horse, he gets better every day," said Miguel.

"I'll let you call off the bet if you want," said Ham.

"Make it ten," said Miguel.

One evening when Willie went off to a Chaplin's meeting at the rec hall Ham got a touch of homesickness, thinking about his mom and his sisters back home in Vermont.

He'd been gone over a month so he started to write a letter on one of the pads he used when he was trying to handicap the races. Before he knew it, he'd filled both sides of three pages, telling about life around the barn and working with the horses and Willie, how much he had learned and how she shouldn't be worried.

He didn't say exactly where he was since he wasn't sure if she would try to make him come home, even though she could probably figure it out, but he knew she had her hands full with his two sisters and the two step-sisters that came with her new husband so he stuck a twenty-dollar bill in for her just to show he was doing well.

You would have thought that Secretariat's race in the Futurity was the only important thing happening in the world that week. Not only was it on the front page of the *Morning Telegraph*, but also every day that week the sports pages of the *New York Times* and the *Herald Tribune* and the *Daily News* and the *New York Post* were all filled with articles about Big Red.

Even stories of an American running first in the Olympic marathon in Germany and a bunch of gold medals in swimming didn't evoke anything close to the excitement that big chestnut colt stirred up.

But when the entries for Saturday came out on the overnight sheet, Ham's eyes didn't go to Secretariat's Futurity but instead right to the last race of the day, a maiden $35,000 claimer, and there it was and it gave him a shiver, Starlight's name in the fifth position on the list of a ten fillies and mares to run the mile race, each looking for the first win of their careers.

Starlight had a dozen starts over the past year and a half, finishing second and third in a few with the same kind and if there wasn't anyone too tough in there, Ham figured she might be able to win. He knew most of the other horses in the race since he'd been keeping an eye on that category, clipping their charts from his found newspapers.

When he showed Willie the overnight, Willie just smiled.

"Wouldn't that be sweet, Ham and Eggs..."

Saturday morning Ham paced the barn like an expectant father waiting on an overdue baby.

"Go on up 'the kitchen, boy, 'git you some breakfast," said Willie, "You gonna make that horse crazy, 'y'all keep messing with him."

Ham knew Willie was right, so he fetched his *Morning Telegraph* from the foot box and when he got his bacon, egg and cheese on a hard roll he headed to a corner table so he could handicap Starlight's race for the fourteenth time. It was a race for maidens, those horses that have never won a race and once they win they can never run with maidens again.

The '1' and '2' horses were both three year-old fillies making their debut for trainers who didn't ever seem to have their horses ready to crack first time out. The next was a four year old like Starlight, but she'd had plenty of chances and never been close with horses even weaker than these. The '4' horse looked like the likely favorite to Ham since she'd been a decent second in her last start, only losing by a few lengths, but she wanted to run late and he reckoned her lack of speed would put her too far back to be a real threat.

Mister Evans was putting blinkers on Starlight for the first time Saturday, saying he didn't know why he'd waited so long and that she needed to get her mind on business and stop messing around before she ended up an old maid.

The '6' was another closer, one who'd had a few starts and probably would go off second choice just because of her changing to the girl jockey, Robyn Smith. She had super-model good looks and since lots of folks had seen her kisser on the cover of *Sports Illustrated* Ham figured they'd bet her odds down, but the horse was slow and he didn't think she had a shot.

The rest of the horses in the race looked ordinary, nothing special about a bunch whose best finish was eighth, all of them beaten ten or twelve lengths. So Starlight would be there in the middle, the one with some lick and getting blinkers, the only one with speed and right in between two slow-poke starters that would have to come from way behind. The way Ham saw it, Woodhouse would gun her out of there, make a big lead and if she didn't get pressed by one of the firsters she might be able to steal the show.

Like Willie said, "Wouldn't that be sweet..."

He finished his sandwich and washed it down with a soda, folded up the Telly and shoved his hand in the pocket of his jeans, touching the wad of cash he planned to bet and when he stood up his head swam a bit and he had a lofty feeling, like he was a couple of feet taller than the folks around him and looking down on his surroundings and just as quickly the feeling was gone.

When he got back to the barn, Willie was fooling with the television in Mister Evan's office, trying to get a clear picture by squeezing some aluminum foil on the rabbit-ear antenna.

"Probably work better if we put it outside," said Ham, and Willie grinned, knowing he was right.

They set the little black and white up on a couple of bales of straw outside the shedrow so anyone who had to stay at the barn could see the great Secretariat run.

By the middle of the afternoon Ham had been back to the kitchen half-a-dozen times and over to the frontside once to get an overnight, even though he knew they didn't have anything entered.

Willie came in Starlight's stall and showed Ham how to braid her mane, just for something to occupy the boy's mind. And then they sat outside, watching the TV commentators, the man with the hat and trench coat and the pretty girl that had an accent kind of like Willie's, knowing that the call to the paddock would come soon and they'd be walking Starlight over while Secretariat's race was run and the most they could expect was to hear the announcer's voice and the roar of the crowd.

Ham wore an almost new shirt, one he'd bought just for the times when he would run a horse, proud to wear the same color red as Mister Evan's silks. Willie told him it was bad luck to wear new when you had a runner, so he had washed it a couple of times as not to take any chances.

Ham blushed when Mister Evans made that same comment about the beauty show and he saw Willie's chest swell, hearing him get the compliment. They stood on the grandstand apron in the same spot they did when they watched Delilah win and as the horses approached the starting gate, way across the track, Ham's stomach hurt and he felt a bit dizzy.

Starlight went to her knees as the gate opened, maybe because the ground broke away, and the jockey had to send her hard to pass the ones in front and by the time they turned for home she had made the lead and opened up a couple of lengths. Ham was wanting to yell but nothing would come out of his dry mouth, so he just pulled on Willie's sleeve and whispered:

"Please..."

Getting left at the gate usually costs a horse something and Starlight got just the tiniest bit tired those last few yards, so when the favorite lunged forward their noses hit the wire together.

Ham was panting like a long distance runner as he and Willie waited at the rail for the horses to come back, unable to take their eyes from the red "PHOTO" sign lit on the tote board.

All the other horses got unsaddled except Starlight and the favorite and they both circled on the track waiting, until the light went out and Ham's knees buckled slightly and he let out a grunt, not wanting Willie to hear him swear as the favorite's number went up, first to Starlight's second.

Evening light was fading fast as Ham finished doing Starlight up and he was sitting in the straw at her feet with his back to the stall door when he heard a voice say,

"Here you go," and he turned to see Miguel's outstretched hand with the ten-dollar bill.

"I forgot about it," said Ham, "I even forgot to bet on Starlight."

"We got closer this time," said Miguel. "Make it twenty for the next one."

"It's your money," said Ham. "Better you give it to me than some stranger."

Miguel made an obscene gesture and laughed as he said the same insult in Spanish that he always did when they were kidding each other.

"And I saw your man today, the little bug from Saratoga."

"Who?" said Ham.

"Spider, all dressed up and he said he's going to be a jockey," said Miguel.

CHAPTER 3

Ham walked Buckeye toward Mister Evans and Doc Kennery on the hard dirt road between the barns.

"Jog him," said Evans and Ham did.

"Faster, son," said the vet.

Buckeye was almost pulling Ham off the ground when they got to the two men and he was thankful that the big bay had pulled himself up rather than run them over.

"Good with me," said Doc, "That's the soundest I've ever seen him.

"Put him away," said Evans, nodding agreement.

Ham led Buckeye back to his stall and was dusting him off with a rub-rag when the trainer came to the door.

"I'm going to enter him to run on Friday, Ham," he said.

"Yessir," said Ham.

"If he gets in, we'll breeze him an easy half tomorrow and keep our fingers crossed."

"Yessir," said Ham.

On the way back from supper at the track kitchen Ham swung by the rec hall to get an overnight and check if anyone had abandoned a *Morning Telegraph* but there were none of either to be found, just the same bunch of trainers and jockey agents that were always there playing race horse rummy, so he headed to the stable gate and got the entries from the guard.

He shivered when he saw Buckeye's name listed in the second race for Friday, a $35,000 maiden claimer like the one Starlight ran in, only this was for colts and geldings, and seven furlongs instead of six. That meant they'd be taking him to the track at dawn tomorrow as soon as it opened so he could have a nice smooth track for his workout.

When Ham showed Willie the overnight, the old man grinned from ear to ear.

"That's a man amongst boys 'you be running there, Ham and Eggs," he said.

Ham figured he meant because Buckeye had cost so much and said so and Willie told him he was right, plus Buckeye's father was a big-time stallion and his mother a stakes-winning mare, both things that Ham wasn't aware of since pedigree was something he'd just started to learn.

"His daddy First Landing sired the Derby winner last May. 'Ought to be enough to make him beat them ill-bred rascals," said Willie.

Ham was the first one in the shedrow the next morning, eager to get Buckeye ready for his breeze and he was combing the last bits of straw from the gelding's tail when Jake draped Lizzie's exercise saddle over the webbing at the front of the stall.

He ran his hands over Buckeye's ankles one last time to reassure himself there was no heat and sure enough they were ice cold, just like they had been last night when he put him away. But he'd heard enough stories from Willie about horses that were sound as a dollar one moment and limping lame the next, so he wasn't about to let his guard down.

Mister Evans was quiet on the way to the track, and Lizzie too kept her usual chatter to a minimum, waiting for instructions on how the trainer wanted the workout to go. Ham stroked the big bay on his chest and shoulder as they walked, trying to keep him relaxed although you could tell Buckeye knew something was up, the way horses do when they sense any change in their routine.

"Fifty flat, perfect," said Evans as he clicked his stopwatch.

He clicked it again and winked at Ham as Buckeye galloped past the seven-eighths pole.

"Out in one-oh-three and three... Let's hope he doesn't do anything stupid between now and tomorrow afternoon," said the trainer.

Ham wore his red shirt to the paddock and Toady lugged the bucket since Willie had Momma's Boy running in the third race and he was busy, or he'd have been walking alongside, proud as a papa of his protégé. As they made a couple of laps around the walking ring, Ham snuck a peek at the odds board and had to look again to be sure what he saw up there was right. Buckeye was twelve-to-one, which was much higher a price than he thought he'd be and more than double the morning line odds. Ham wasn't sure what to make of that, but it made him nervous about the forty bucks he planned to bet, twenty to win and twenty to place.

Buckeye was on his toes as the field left the paddock, doing a little buck-jump and making a few owners step back to get out of the way.

"Good luck," said Ham to the rider.

Johnny Mallano was a dark-eyed handsome Italian kid, popular with the fans at Belmont and still only a bug-boy but Ham felt good about him riding Buckeye, figuring he and Mallano were both apprentices and maybe that was why the odds were high, folks preferring to bet on Vasquez or Baeza or Cordero, those guys who won all the big races, but it was okay with him, since like Willie said, everybody had to start someplace.

Ham tucked the tickets in his left front shirt pocket where he always did, getting more and more superstitious like a true racetracker. And he wouldn't let himself look at the odds on the tote board again until the horses went in the gate, thinking of the time Willie told him about when he was running a horse in the Bluegrass Stakes at Keeneland and he'd made the mistake of looking at the trophy before the race and he was sure that was the reason his horse got beat that nose.

Ham and Toady found a spot on the grandstand apron near the fence where they had a clear view of the starting gate at the other side of the track, right where it straightened out for the backstretch. There were a few other first time starters in the race and one of them pitched a fit behind the gate, delaying the start and that didn't help the stomach ache Ham was feeling.

Mallano turned his stick down a hundred yards from the finish line and coasted home about five lengths in front and this time Ham didn't have a dry mouth as he jumped up and screamed "Yee-haw" when they crossed the wire and he and Toady hustled out on to the track to wait for Buckeye.

Ham had that feeling come over him as he stepped on that loamy Belmont track, that he was about a foot or two taller than everyone around him, as if they were all moving in slow motion and speaking strange garbled sounds but he had to move quickly to get his horse and didn't have time to dwell on it.

The jock shook his whip towards the stands and tossed it to his valet, meaning that all was well and when Ham threaded the brass chain of the shank through Buckeye's bridle and led them into the winners circle it was close as to who had a bigger grin, him or that bug boy.

All the time Ham had worked for Mister Evans, he'd never seen the man show even a trace of anger, but right now as the photographer took their picture his face was as red as the jockey's silks and he looked like he might explode when the steward's assistant hung a plastic tag on Buckeye's halter.

It said: "CLAIMED."

An hour later when Ham got back to the barn, all he had was his shank and Buckeye's halter so he was surely relieved to see Willie waiting for him.

"I never even thought about them taking him," said Ham.

"I didn't think they would either," said Willie, "him waiting 'til he's almost five to get to the races, but you never know."

"Mister Evans sure was mad."

"More'n likely that horse just lost his best friend," said Willie, meaning that a maiden was the easiest race for any horse to win and it only got tougher after that and as Ham mulled it over he knew the old man was probably right, but at the moment it stung pretty bad to lose the big gelding that was his very first winner and the one that left him with a scar on his butt.

They went to dinner at the Italian place that night, but it was a nearly silent repast and when they toasted Buckeye it felt more like a wake than a wedding. And although Ham had won a sizeable bet and he was going to miss Buckeye, he could tell Willie was disappointed that Momma's Boy ran out of the money, maybe fearing that the old gelding was getting to the end of his career.

There wasn't much small talk over dinner and after they were done as Ham paid the check he remembered how Willie liked to say a little quiet was good for the soul and that particular evening Ham knew what he meant.

When they got back to the barn there was a letter waiting, stuck in the tack room door. It was addressed to Ham in his mother's handwriting and sent to him in care of the Belmont stable gate, so she had figured out where he was, probably by the postmark on his letter to her.

Mom said everything was good back home in Vermont, that his sisters and his step-sisters were well and that they all missed him and that she was excited that her husband had found a new job, one that might have some future there at the resort which was beginning to prosper since they'd started to promote year-round instead of depending on it to snow for the skiers every winter.

His mom made no mention of him coming home, just told him that she loved him and hoped he was happy there working with the horses and how she'd loved horses too when she was a girl, something he'd never heard from her before but for some reason that gave him a good feeling. He put the letter in an old cigar box where he'd been keeping his losing tickets, not ripping them up and throwing them on the ground like a lot of bettors did.

Willie said it was good to keep some losers around to remind you of the times when you weren't that smart, 'cause when you win you always think you're a genius.

He told himself he'd write again soon, but as a matter of fact it would be a long time before he did.

Ham was in the tack shop, buying himself a pair of those brown leather Kroops boots with the zipper in the front that a lot of folks on the backside wore, when he saw Spider.

"Hey," said Ham.

"Hey," said Spider.

"We all thought you hit the road again after Saratoga," said Ham.

And just like before, Spider didn't look him in the eye as he shrugged. Ham hadn't given it much thought before that moment just how small the kid was, that maybe he wore a size five shoe and probably got his clothes in the boy's section at the department store.

"I heard you were going to be a jockey."

"Yeah, 'working for Bucky Layne," said Spider.

"Cool," said Ham.

Bucky Layne was what Willie called a "gyp" trainer, meaning he always cut corners and did everything as cheaply as he could, even if it meant skimping on things that were good for his horses, which was why they always looked so shabby and undernourished.

Layne didn't care too much what he himself looked like either, always in dirty jeans and a tee-shirt and missing a couple of teeth, and being a wild gambler who bet on every race, whether or not he had a horse in it but seemingly calm except once in a while when his eyes would flash and you could see how he might have been a crazy person.

It was a known fact on the backstretch that Layne and his wife took care of a couple of dozen horses with one groom their only help and Ham figured Spider was working more for promises than he was for money.

"I'm galloping the whole barn," said Spider in a boasting way as if that were a good thing.

But Spider appeared pretty prosperous for someone who probably wasn't making much money, wearing new boots and jeans and a plaid western shirt like a lot of the jockeys did, and paying for a Caliente helmet with a hundred-dollar bill.

Maybe Bucky Layne paid better than Ham thought he did.

"See ya," said Spider, grabbing his change from the counter.

"See ya," said Ham, wondering if a lot of things about Spider didn't add up.

Ham told Evans he didn't think it was right that he got paid the same now as he was only taking care of two horses, that maybe he should take less since one of them was a pony, not even a moneymaker for the barn and the trainer laughed out loud.

"Forty years, I never had anybody tell me they were overpaid," he said.

Later that morning, when Ham busied himself raking the gravel parking lot, the trainer called him into his office.

"We're going to claim one out of the first race," he said, "Meet me at that hedge by the paddock where the horses come in. Bring a shank and a halter and hopefully you'll have another one to rub."

He didn't say which horse they were taking but Ham figured that wasn't his business and he'd better just do what he was told since Willie always liked to say even a fish wouldn't get in trouble if it kept its mouth shut.

Ham stayed close by Evans and strained to listen as the old man spoke behind his cupped hand in a low voice, like he didn't want anyone to hear them. The trainer was focused on the path from the barn area, making notes on his program and seeming to check out every horse, but when a big grey mare appeared, practically dragging her groom into the walking ring, he nudged Ham.

"That's her," he said, "...Avalanche."

"Yessir," said Ham.

"Got those front bandages on 'trying to make you think they're hiding something, but I've been watching her on the track in the morning and she's sound, let's go " he said.

Ham followed him to the racing secretary's office and he showed Ham the claim blank he'd filled out before he put it in the envelope and stuck it in the machine that stamped it with the time and dropped it in the slot in a wooden box with a lock on it. They weren't alone in the room and stood aside while they watched three other trainers do the same thing.

"Looks like we're going to shake for her," said Evans.

Ham knew the claiming race was like an auction, that anyone who put up the money would be buying the horse, but he didn't know what it meant to shake for one so he asked.

"They put numbered pills in a cup and if your number comes out first, your claim's the one that gets her."

The claims clerk put the three blanks side by side on the counter and said:

"One is Evans, two is Burke and three is Colletti. Good luck, gentlemen."

He shook the cup and out rolled a red pill with the number '1' and Mister Evans perked up with a smile. He took the receipt from the clerk and passed it to Ham as overhead on the television the horses broke from the gate.

The grey mare flew to the front and was still up by four when she passed the finish line.

Ham felt a little uneasy, waiting at the test barn while Avalanche's groom finished walking her, but when he was done, Ham handed the receipt to the man in charge and headed back to the Evans stable with his new horse. Halfway there she planted her feet and he could have sworn she was looking him up and down as if she was deciding whether or not to like him.

He reached in his pocket and pulled out the peppermint Willie had given him before he went to the paddock.

"All the girls like it when you bring them candy," Willie had said, and there he was waiting with Mister Evans as they got to the barn and when they went over their new horse she was clean and sound and healthy as could be.

"Not a pimple on her," said the trainer.

"Sound as a bell of brass," said Willie.

And Ham thought about it as he put Avalanche in her new stall, how many times he'd heard those same words, even in the short time he'd been around, and how the race track world had its own language, full of quirky expressions and how much he loved to hear them.

Since Chester was a working pony and Mister Evans spent most of the time riding him back and forth to the track, Ham would have him ready first thing with the big western saddle on and tied to the hitching post outside. Most mornings Evans liked to just sit there by the half-mile gap on the big palomino, clocking horses with an old gold stopwatch he'd won for being the leading trainer at Latonia which was an old track in Kentucky where he said he'd helped Eddie Arcaro get his start as a jockey. He said they didn't make them like Arcaro any more, and Willie agreed, saying that was why they called him "the Master."

Avalanche had raced the day before, so she didn't go to the track and Ham just walked her, first in the shedrow for a while, then outside on the walking ring, getting her used to the new surroundings and she was perfect. She'd had white rings around her eyes when they came back last night and did spook a few times and when he mentioned it to Mister Evans he said that likely the other trainer had lit her up with a cattle prod at the barn before the race, something he didn't approve of and in his barn they'd be treating her like a lady, not some Angus steer.

Ham had just put the mare back in her stall and was coming back from the feed room after fetching her some alfalfa when a loose horse came wheeling around the corner and ducked into the shedrow and it was a good thing he was looking or he'd have gotten run over. Instead, he dropped the flake of hay and grabbed the dangling reins, and walked the horse outside to hand her off to Jake.

"Lizzie got dumped," said Jake.

"Is she okay?" said Ham.

"Ambulance took her," said Jake, shrugging.

It wasn't that far to the hospital but Ham put on a clean shirt and took the bus instead of borrowing a bike from one of the other grooms, as he didn't want to get sweaty. He got some flowers at the gift shop and the lady at the information desk asked him if they were for his wife, which embarrassed him considerably but when he got to her room Lizzie wasn't there. It was a two-bedded room and there was an old lady watching television, her eyes glued to *As the World Turns*.

"I'm looking for my friend Lizzie," said Ham.

"She was out cold until about an hour ago," said the lady, "They just took her for an x-ah-ray."

Ham was pretty sure that wasn't good.

"Is she okay?"

"Looked okay to me," said the lady.

Ham woke with a start when Lizzie's gurney bumped the door as it came into the room. He had no idea how long he'd been asleep in the chair but the old lady was gone from the other bed and her television was dark.

"Aren't you sweet," said Lizzie when she saw the flowers.

"How do you feel?" said Ham.

"Got a little headache, but I'm okay," she said, "I was on the Never Bend filly, the two year old, and she jumped the fence I guess. I don't really remember."

"Out cold, they said."

"I needed that nap," she said, "And so did you."

Lizzie looked well enough although she still had a smudge of track dirt on her face and he didn't want to let on how concerned he'd been.

"They say the food is great in these places."

"Yeah," she said, "people throw themselves off horses just to get in here."

Before he could ask, she told him they were making her stay overnight and when he said he could stop back later she said perhaps he would bring her a few things from Tina, the other exercise girl she lived with. They had an apartment not far from the track and Tina was home nursing a broken leg so she wouldn't be able to come over and Ham said sure, see you later.

"Thanks for the flowers, darlin," she said and he blushed.

The Champagne Stakes at Belmont is usually the biggest race of the year for two year olds, often the one that makes the champion and there was no doubt that Secretariat would be just that and maybe, like a lot of folks said, he'd be the Horse of the Year although that honor almost always went to older horses.

If the press had been crazy for Big Red before the Futurity, now they were certifiably insane and Willie said if Secretariat was running for President next month Nixon and McGovern would both be fighting for second place.

Every day when Stop the Music went to the track to gallop, the path Miguel took home brought them right past the Evans barn. Usually grooms didn't walk each of their horses back and forth to the track, but in the case of stars like Secretariat and aspiring ones like Stop the Music, the trainer would take no chances and have them do it just to insure nothing went wrong.

Miguel would whistle to Ham when they passed, then sing a few lines of his favorite song; "*Bye-bye, Miss American Pie... 'drove my Chevy to the levee but the levee was dry...*" and Willie and Ham would laugh at that boy for thinking there was any way his horse was going to get by Secretariat.

The Wednesday before the Champagne marked two months since Hamilton Greer's sixteenth birthday, the day he climbed on a Greyhound bus in Manchester, Vermont, and in his mind he marked that as the day he became a man. He had himself a little money saved now, hidden and secure, and he dressed himself well in the new clothes he had bought and every two weeks he went over to the grandstand barber shop and got his hair cut like he thought a man should if he expected folks to respect him.

He listened when Willie gave him advice, liking the way it was done, not didactic or preachy or talking down to him, just man to man, or perhaps like father to son, and always spoken in a kindly manner, so he took that advice to heart and remembered it when he was trying to behave properly.

"The Constitution only gives people the right to pursue happiness. You have to catch it yourself," said Willie, "Mister Ben Franklin said that. And there's some things you can get taught, but most you gonna learn for yourself from just living."

After he cashed his bet on Buckeye, Ham went to an appliance store over in Elmont and bought a transistor radio for Willie, and he told him it was how he'd like to show his appreciation for all the things Willie taught him, and for what he hoped he'd teach him in the future, and the old man's eyes were wet when he said thank you.

Because they have to be up so early, racetrackers hit the sack early so they got in the habit of listening to the radio every evening, or if Willie went out for a meeting or Ham went to a movie at the rec hall, the one who stayed in would listen and tell the other what he'd missed and mostly it was news, from all the parts of the other world outside the stable gate they'd never otherwise know about.

Sometimes when Willie dozed off early, Ham would tune it down low and listen to Jean Shepherd tell him stories until he fell asleep too.

A week later Jake hung Ivan's saddle over the webbing as Ham was putting polo bandages on Starlight and Ham asked him why Lizzie wasn't getting on her like she usually did.

"Lizzie's gone, back to England I think," Jake said.

"When?" said Ham.

"Immigration got her last night, they must have figured out she didn't have papers when she was in the hospital."

"So she's gone? Just like that?"

"Deported. Happens all the time," said Jake, "Too bad, she was a good rider."

Ivan took the mare to gallop and Ham went and knocked on the open door of Evans' office and asked him if there was anything anyone could do about Lizzie and he was a loss at what more to say when the trainer told him no but he'd hired a new rider to be there in the morning, just like he didn't even care if she was gone.

Ham moped around the rest of the day, reading and listening to the radio in the tack room and Willie told him don't you worry son, those pretty girls are like buses, if you stand on the corner long enough another one will come by and Ham thought that was a little cold.

Neither had anything running on Saturday, so Willie and Ham got to the paddock right after the sixth race so they could get a spot near the rail in order to be close by when the trainer gave Turcotte a leg up on Secretariat.

All the parking lots off Hempstead Turnpike were overflowing and banner planes above were dragging signs that read; "GO BIG RED," and folks pressed through the turnstiles dressed to the nines like they were going to the biggest party ever, the men all wearing suits and some of the ladies with hats that matched their dresses.

Ham caught Miguel's eye as he passed, giving Stop the Music an extra turn around the walking ring and the dapples on the big bay's hindquarters were shining like translucent mirrors in the afternoon sun.   Miguel gave Ham a "thumbs-up," as proud as a peacock but when the paddock judge yelled "riders-up" Miguel's smile disappeared, meaning he was all business.

The trainer's assistant gave Johnny Rotz a leg up and Willie said how good they looked, the flashy colt with his rider in the bright pink and black silks.

As the horses left the paddock, hardly anyone paid attention to Angle Light, the number '1' horse since all eyes were on Secretariat wearing '1A' on his saddle towel because he was part of an entry, both horses trained by the same trainer. Willie said he thought it was a waste of the other horse, and that Secretariat didn't need what he called a "rabbit" to go out and force a fast pace.

"That big horse can run down anything they put in front of him, going fast or slow," he said.

Ham thought maybe they would have a bet today since Secretariat's odds were hanging around even money, but Willie said just you wait boy, he's gonna be three-to-five and we don't bet no three-to-fives, but when Willie went to the men's room Ham slipped over to the hundred-dollar window and bought a ticket, figuring that would be the easiest way he ever got to double his money.

With a furlong left it looked to be only a matter of how far Big Red would win by and Ham didn't pay much attention to Willie's grunt when Secretariat ducked in on Miguel's horse as he made his run from last, passing the other horses like they were a picket fence. And when he crossed the finish line two lengths clear of Stop the Music, Ham whooped along with the crowd.

But Willie didn't whoop, instead he pointed at the tote board as the red lights lit up on the "INQUIRY" sign.

Ham touched the shirt pocket where he always stashed his tickets and had that dreamy, slow motion thing again, feeling big and sounds garbled while the lights on the result board were dark for a few minutes before they lit again, and the number '5' was up there on top and '1A' in second and he heard the announcer saying:

"...by disqualification... 'winner of the hundred and first running of the Champagne Stakes... Stop the Music, a bay colt by Hail to Reason out of Bebopper, by Tom Fool..." before his voice tailed off.

Walking back to the stable area Willie said it was a dang shame, the stewards taking down the best horse, but that was why we don't bet no horse alive at three-to-five and Ham knew that Willie knew he'd bet his money.

CHAPTER 4

Ham thought it was a funny thing, the way those horsemen at Belmont acted as soon as that first frost hit and right away they all started talking about Florida.

Since he came from a place where everybody's favorite joke was that Vermont is nine months of winter and three months of bad skiing, he was fine with cold weather but apparently at Belmont it was considered a sign from God to pack up and head south.

They were at the rail watching Avalanche breeze and the morning was chilly enough that they could see their breath when Evans announced:

"Hialeah barn area's open now, but we'll give them another week to break that track in, then you and Willie go on the first van."

Willie seemed more than a little pleased that they'd be going early this year, saying that the boss usually waited until after Thanksgiving before shipping south, but he's getting some miles on him too and maybe he wants some warm Florida sunshine on those achy old bones.

"Best place for a horse I 'ever been. Sometimes you take one to Hialeah sore, and pretty soon he's sound. Prettiest place too, 'except I never been to Santa Anita, but I hear that's top class too."

He said Evans liked to drop off some of the horses at a farm in Camden, South Carolina for the winter off, ones that were tired from racing hard all year and needed some time to unwind, and he'd bring some others to run a time or two at Tropical Park and prep for their stakes races before the meet started at Hialeah in January.

Willie said you could always see some of the great runners there at Hialeah, like Bald Eagle and Citation and Bold Ruler and Nashua and great trainers too, like Woody Stephens and Sunny Jim Fitzsimmons and Horatio Luro and Jimmy Jones, everybody beating the cold winter up north and it don't get any better than that on this earth

Miguel laughed when Ham gave him the twenty-dollar bill and he folded it twice and kissed it before stashing the cash in his hatband.

"Doesn't seem right to take your money," he said, "but it's better you give it to me than some stranger."

"I guess you don't want to double-or-nothing next time," said Ham and Miguel just shook his head and laughed some more.

"I don't think anybody <u>ever</u> beats that big red horse again," said Miguel, "We're going to chase him for second money one more time down in Maryland, then take a vacation. There's always next year and plenty of races he won't be in."

Willie was heading to the washroom when Evans waved him over and motioned toward Mighty's stall where the big bay stood quietly, his head hung out over the webbing as he picked at some alfalfa and appraised the two men.

"That's the best horse I've ever had the privilege of laying my hands on, Will."

"That's two of us, sir," said Willie.

"He might be what we waited for, all these years."

"The two of us, sir, yes sir that's right."

It was just two weeks later when Willie had the little black and white television working pretty well in the boss' office, tin foil squeezed on the rabbit-ear antennas and a box at the ready for it to travel south with them the next morning.

"Ten minutes to post," said Willie as on the screen tiny horses and riders broke from the post parade.

"We should have bet," said Ham, making a lame joke since Secretariat was going in the gate as the one-to-nine favorite.

The other grooms and anyone else around the barn on that Saturday afternoon were jammed into the room and they all whistled and cheered when Big Red looped the field and splashed home eight in front over the sloppy track at Laurel Park. Miguel's colt ran a clear second again and Willie said that Stop the Music sure is a nice colt but too bad for him he came along the same year as the one bound for greatness.

Their van pulled into the farm in South Carolina a few minutes past midnight and they unloaded the horses and turned them out in small paddocks for a while to let them loosen up from the standing they'd been doing for the last dozen or so hours since they crossed the George Washington bridge and rolled down the New Jersey Turnpike.

The air had a smell of sulphur and Ham said he thought that was some awful loud crickets chirping but Willie told him those were frogs in the wetlands and set your alarm, son, 'cause we ain't getting much sleep tonight.

When Ham checked his grandpa's pocket watch it read a quarter to five as they led their six horses and two others back onto the same van. That was the time they needed to be going for the driver to make it to Hialeah before dark.

He stood on a bucket at the side window, watching the cars and the countryside go by as the sun came up in swampy north Georgia and he told Willie that was some creepy stuff hanging on those trees and asked are there any alligators out there.

"Spanish moss," said Willie, "and that what's up top there, that's mistletoe, the same stuff you kiss your girlfriends under at Christmas time and believe me, that alligator meat tastes just like chicken if you fry it up in some butter and bread crumbs."

The two vans turned into the Hialeah barn area just as a pile of fluffy clouds in the western sky turned a bright pink, backlit by the setting sun.

Foreman Jake was there at the barn waiting for them along with Penn the feed man who came by to make sure his help had done a good job of bedding the stalls and he called out Willie's name as Willie led Mighty into the shedrow.

"About time you showed up," he said, "Now we can get the winter started."

"You ain't kidding nobody, boss... you 'just been waiting on my shrimp gumbo," said Willie, laughing.

"Damn," said Penn, "You always see right through me, Willie."

Penn told Ham that Willie made the best southern style cooking he'd ever tasted but Ham had never seen Willie cook anything except canned soup so it made him wonder how many other things about him he didn't know.

They unloaded the rest of the traps, which was what they called the barn equipment and put their personal belongings in the tack room and when they were done, Willie told Ham to wash up, they were going out to dinner for a change.

"Easy's taking us down to the Cuban place on Palm Avenue. 'Always better when you 'got somebody can speak the language," said Willie.

"Easy" was what they called Isidro the night watchman, who was probably older than Willie, and while most of his black hair was touched with snowy white, his dark eyes sparkled like those of a young man going out on the town. But he turned serious when he told his friends how glad he was to see them show up, not only because he'd missed them, but also since it meant the good racing was about to begin.

Easy was a chatty guy and it seemed as if he never stopped talking long enough for a deep breath as they crossed Palm Avenue to the little restaurant with the white and blue shutters and red awnings and the whole time Ham nodded to be polite, since he couldn't understand a word the old Cuban said, so fractured was his English, mixed with Spanish words.

The dark haired girl at the door kissed Easy and Willie on the cheek and hugged them each and when she held out her hand to meet Ham, he felt himself flush but he tried to shrug it off when they got to the table and the two old men teased him.

They let Easy do the ordering and the food looked strange to Ham, especially the things Willie told him were a kind of bananas but he had never tasted pork with onions and rice and black beans like that before and would have thought it was the best place he'd ever eaten even if that dark haired girl didn't smile at him every time their eyes met.

While they were in New York, Evans' daughter Mary had been his assistant, but in the winter she'd go to South Carolina to be with the two year olds where she'd watch to see which ones took to early training and she could judge which of those would be first to come to the track in the Spring.

Mister Evans didn't trust airplanes and he'd take his time driving down and on the way he'd stop by to check with Mary, so every winter at Hialeah he put an old horseman called Bogie in charge until he got there.

The assistant trainer's real name was Edgar Alexander and he was from Chicago, but when he spoke lots of folks thought he sounded like the movie star and that racetrack name had hung on him for the past forty years.

Willie told Bogie that Ham was a smart kid and even if he was a new hand, you could trust him with a nice horse and Bogie just nodded and said nothing, like he was taking that under consideration. A couple of days later he had Jake move Chester the pony to another groom and gave Ham a lanky filly named Suzie's Song that didn't look like much but must have been a runner since Willie said she had won a stakes race last year at Hialeah.

"Better watch that chestnut hussy," said Willie, "She thinks she's the toughest thing in town, and when she's horsin' she might try to eat you."

"Horsin'?" said Ham.

"'Means when they come in season, 'like a dog when it's in heat, needing to get bred and sometimes when you think they're going to run good they run bad and that's the reason why."

"Mister Evans must have told Bogie you're a ladies' man, 'giving you all them fillies," said Easy and Ham got a kick out of the way the old guys kidded him, thinking maybe they halfway imagined he was a young version of them, back in the days when they still chased the girls.

There were only two ways to take the horses to the Hialeah track for training, either through the parking lot to the quarter pole gap which was the shorter way from the

Evans barn or down the horse path, a broad colonnade of tall Australian pines that bordered the back of the barns. The pines had long needles that made a soft swishing sound when even the mildest breeze blew and it seemed like that relaxed the horses, and even the nervous ones would drop their heads and let out a deep breath.

Whichever way they went out, they returned the other and Bogie would let Ham come along whenever one of his horses would go to breeze.

As they walked through the paddock Bogie told him about the famous track in France that the building was modeled after and that the coral it was built from was cut from the reefs and came out of the ocean right there off Miami, back in the days when you could do that but now it's protected so you'll never see anything like this again.

Ham would often head back to those stands in the afternoon where he would sit alone and eat a sandwich while a guy in a canoe roused the flock of flamingos to flight and they circled over the track a couple of times before landing on an island in the center of the lake to have their own lunch.

A week or so passed and still Mister Evans hadn't shown up, but Bogie went on training the horses, liking to get them all out to the track in the first morning light, not allowing any to train in the heat of the day or the "thick air" which was what he called the South Florida humidity.

But if a front from Canada with some cool breezes should sweep through for a few days he would do just the opposite and take them all out late in order to avoid those horses that felt so good that they dumped their riders and ran loose until the outriders could catch them.

And he liked to take the horses out in sets of four or five, all the riders lining up at the outside fence and sitting still for a few minutes before they urged their mounts on, Bogie saying that they'd get more out of their training if they were relaxed and well behaved.

The old man had a lot of tricks like that and rarely gave an explanation of what he was doing when he was doing it, but that was part of what made the work so interesting for Ham, that he could watch and try and figure it out for himself before he asked. And when he did come by the office, Bogie had all the time in the world for him, happy to teach, and Ham happy to listen, as he imagined himself playing a role in a Hollywood movie about the racetrack, exchanging lines with the movie's star.

Suzy's Song had been turned out at the farm in South Carolina for the past six months and Willie said the boss liked to do that with some horses, give them a break so they'd be fresh at a track where they had run well before, what he called "horses for courses." The farm trainer would get them galloping along and maybe breeze them a few times and Bogie would just have to tune them up, kind of like tightening the strings on a guitar.

When a jock from the Windy City named Earlie Fires showed up at dawn to get on Suzie's Song, it seemed that he and Bogie knew each other so well that they could finish each other's sentences. Ham just listened as they made small talk while they walked the filly from the barn, across the parking lot, out to the quarter pole gap and onto the track.

Bogie and Ham climbed the grandstand steps to the box seats where the clockers sat and Bogie pulled out his stopwatch and handed Ham his spare as the jockey jogged Suzie's Song clockwise to the finish line, what everybody called the "wrong way," because when horses race they go counter-clockwise and that's the "right way." Fires turned the filly around and let her stand for a moment to catch her breath before he eased her along down the backstretch and picked up speed as they dropped to the rail.

"Click the top button when she passes the half-mile pole and the side one when she passes the three-eighths. You need to click it a stride before she gets there, kind of lead her," said the old man.

"Okay," said Ham, and when he heard Bogie's click he knew he was late for the first pole, having not led the filly enough.

"Might take a few times to get it," said Bogie, but when Suzie zipped by the next pole, their watches clicked in unison and the old man just nodded and winked.

"Thirty five and one, she went," Ham told Willie when they got back to the barn.

"She gets ready quick, 'always do," said Willie.

Willie told Ham he figured Bogie was preparing Suzie's Song ready for a race when the boss arrived on Thanksgiving, and sure enough, the next morning Bogie leaned in the stall doorway and told Ham just that.

"Big day coming up, young man," said Willie, "Your first stakes race."

Bogie sent Ham to the racing office to turn in the horses' foal papers and a bundle of jockey's silks for the ones that were ready to run at Tropical. The foal papers looked like stock certificates, edged with fancy engraving and pressed with an official looking seal from The Jockey Club and he held them up in the light to see the watermark.

As he left the office, Ham asked a clerk for some old condition books to use when he packed Avalanche's feet in mud and he grabbed a current one from the counter on the way out so he could try and guess where Mister Evans and Bogie would enter his horses.

There in the parking lot was Spider, leaning on a new red Camaro Super Sport.

"Hey," said Ham.

"Hey," said Spider.

"Still with Layne?" said Ham.

Spider shook his head.

"He worked my ass off and then shipped back to Oklahoma and stiffed me," said Spider.

Ham asked who he was working for and Spider gave him a cold stare as an older man got in the passenger side.

"I'm working for me," said Spider, sliding into the car.

"See ya," said Ham.

The week before Thanksgiving Ham still hadn't run a horse, nor had Willie, but everything was galloping sound and their workouts couldn't have been any better.

On a couple of occasions they took the bus, once to Miami Beach to have a look at the Atlantic ocean which Ham had never seen, but they didn't stay long since Ham was fair-skinned and just wanted to jump in once so he could say he did and another time Easy took them to Calle Ocho where a lot of his Cuban friends lived and Ham watched as his two old men smoked cigars at the park while they watched a lot of other old men play dominoes.

At the far end of the stable area was a maintenance yard where the crew kept their tractors and harrows and the trucks they used for watering the racetrack. And there was a basketball court in the yard like the one at Belmont and some evenings Ham and Willie would walk down to shoot some hoops before the sun went down.

Willie told Ham about how he'd been pretty good at that game when he was a kid, played on a team in high school and even thought it might he might be good enough for college and Ham said he almost joined the team at his school until he overheard the coach make a remark about his mother and punched the jerk in the mouth, and that was part of why he'd left home.

On Sunday evenings Easy and Ham would help Willie set up his kitchen outside the barn, a pair of propane burners and a long folding table, but that was where he'd cook his famous shrimp gumbo from a recipe he said an old Cajun lady gave him the winter he worked at the Fair Grounds track in New Orleans. They put it over white rice and never was there ever a single bite left over.

"How come you didn't cook at Saratoga?" said Ham.

"It's just something I do in a couple of places," said Willie, "and that's what makes it special. If you do something all the time, it loses its specialness and becomes ordinary."

And once in a while Penn the feed man brought the corn bread to go with Willie's fried chicken and hush puppies and collard greens and breaded okra that came from a slave recipe he said his mama got from her mama and after they ate Toady and his brother played guitar and sang some country ballads their daddy taught them when they were kids back in Tennessee.

Ham was beginning to think that Bogie might be holding back from entering the horses, waiting for Mister Evans to arrive when Bogie told him he was entering Avalanche in an allowance race going six furlongs.

Tropical Park was a ways south of Hialeah, so the horses all had to van over on the morning of the race. Willie said he liked it well enough at the little track but word was this would be the last season they ran there, closing up for good to become a county park, a picnic spot for families.

Willie rode with Ham and Avalanche and even though she was in the seventh race, they took the early van and when the grey mare was settled in the receiving barn, they went over to the grandstand to watch a few races.

Ham said the track was cute, which made Willie laugh and he agreed that its grandstand was modest compared to Saratoga and Hialeah with their broad open spaces and rows and rows of seats and it felt downright tiny next to the behemoth Belmont that could hold fifty thousand people without feeling crowded. Willie said most racetrackers would have called Tropical a "bullring" for being only seven furlongs around, except for the fact that plenty of good horses ran there, which they didn't at the other bullrings.

And it did feel more like a county fair than the other places Ham had seen and Willie said lots of folks thought it was just a story that the horses once had to jump an alligator when it wandered out of the infield lake on to the track right in the middle of a race but Easy told him he had been there and seen it happen and he swore it was true.

Ham made a couple of two dollar bets on horses he knew from up north that he thought looked like easy winners, but none of them even hit the board and Willie shook his head and said you should think twice before doing that with your hard earned money.

"They're only here practicing, getting ready for the big money at the next meet and if it isn't a money race they don't try too hard," said Willie,

"Don't waste your bullets, shooting at sparrows. 'Plenty big fat turkeys to aim for at the next town."

There were so many jockeys at Tropical that most of them hardly got one or two mounts except for maybe Jacinto Vasquez who was leading rider, mainly off all the stakes races he won and even he only had half-a-dozen rides each day.

The Tropical paddock was about a quarter of the size of the one at Belmont, and Ham felt like everything about the place was a miniature version of Big Sandy. But the trainers and the jockeys and horses went through the same routine they did at Belmont and Saratoga, saddling in the stalls and circling the walking ring until the Paddock Judge yelled "Riders-up!" and off they went through the tunnel to the track.

It seemed like the grey mare was five in front as soon as the gate opened and Willie said that jock Fires might be the best he'd ever seen at putting one on the lead. As they passed the quarter pole he still hadn't moved his hands and Avalanche no doubt appreciated the fact that he never touched her once with his whip.

Willie went back to the grandstand to cash their tickets while Ham took Avalanche to the spit barn for her winner's test. Willie said that was a sign of respect for trainers like Evans and Bogie that they only got five to one, that the punters would back a horse that hadn't been out in a month and moving up in class besides running first time for a new barn.

The first win at a new meet is seen to portend good luck to come as it brings huge relief from the prospect of getting shut out, which every barn fears more than anything, what Willie called getting the rubber duck.

Bogie got all the barn help to come to dinner at the Cuban restaurant that night, telling them they had to because it was family supper time and most everyone came, including Jake the foreman and all the hotwalkers and grooms and Ivan, who was the only exercise rider that lived at the barn in a tack room.

When it was time to pay for the feast of pork and chicken and black beans and rice and plantains, Bogie grabbed the check and made a little speech, saying how much he appreciated them all and that he thought they were as good a team as the Miami Dolphins, the team he said was going to win the Super Bowl in a couple of months.

Secretariat won his final race of the season in the Futurity at Garden State Park that Saturday and earned himself a trip home to Virginia for a vacation, taking along the winner's share of the biggest purse of the year.

Ham said it was a shame they missed seeing it on television, but taking care of the home team was more important, and like Bogie had said, they were a strong team at the Evans barn, and when Mighty got to running, there was no telling what kind of year they'd have.

And as his head lay on the pillow that night, Ham barely moved while he dreamed of herd of mustangs on a vast plain, a single white horse running alone, far ahead of the pack.

CHAPTER 5

The Sunday before Thanksgiving marked the end of their first month in Florida, and Bogie was still saying that the boss would arrive any day now.

Willie wondered out loud why it would take the man so long to drive himself down from New York but hopefully he was buying some horses off the farms in South Carolina to stock up the stable for next year and that was probably what it was.

Suzie's Song was entered in the stakes race at Tropical Park on Thanksgiving Day and it put Ham on needles and pins when he bought the *Morning Telegraph* and saw that she was picked as favorite by most of the handicappers, and best bet of the day by a few. Even worse, they had her picture on the front page.

Bogie gave Suzie a quarter-mile blowout that Wednesday and he had Ivan do it, saying she was so sharp he didn't want to risk having her run off with some light-weight jockey.

At seven a.m. on Thanksgiving morning Mister Evans pulled up to the barn and right away you could tell he wasn't himself. His usual ruddy complexion had turned a waxen pale and he moved gingerly down the shedrow with Bogie as he went over every horse from their nose to their tail while he listened to what each groom had to say.

Ham could read the concern on Willie's face when the pair got to their end of the barn, but at least Evans cracked a smile when he saw the shining coats on their horses, dapples scattered like shiny silver dollars on Deliah and Starlight and Suzie and Avalanche and he stepped right into Mighty's stall to run his hands over the big bay.

"Lovely," was all Evans said with a weak voice they'd never heard before.

After he left they were packing their gear to take on the van to Tropical and when Ham went to tie his shoe, the lace snapped off in his hand.

"Damn," said Willie.

They took the early van to Tropical again and at the receiving barn Willie told Ham to put the brass chain of his shank over the top of Suzie's front teeth, saying that feeling it on her gums would make her pay attention and not get rowdy in the paddock and it was a good thing he did, because when Ham took the filly out of her stall, she halfway dragged him down the shedrow until he gave a stern yank to stop her in her tracks.

"Good as hands can make her, son," said Willie, "You done a man's job with this filly."

When they circled the paddock, Suzy pranced like one of those fancy dressage horses in Madison Square Garden, and she stood as still as a statue as Bogie gave Fires his leg up. But Mister Evans was nowhere to be seen.

"Good luck, jock," said Ham.

Fires winked and tucked his whip under his leg as he pulled out some of the rubber bands in her braided mane while they moved on toward the tunnel that led out to the racetrack.

Suzie's odds flirted with four-to-five and she was going to go in the gate at no better than even money in the field of ten, which made it a non-betting situation for them, so Ham and Willie grabbed a lemonade and just watched from the grandstand apron as the horses came out of the gate at the three-quarter pole chute.

But instead of being on the lead where she was supposed to be, their filly wasn't in front of a single horse as they ran the first quarter-mile, and when the field turned for home there was no doubt that she was going to be last.

Bogie waited with them as Fires waved his whip and dismounted.

"What happened?" said Bogie and the jock just shrugged his shoulders and said she was sound, hitting the ground perfect but didn't give an ounce of effort.

"I didn't want to beat her up for nothing," he said.

Ham didn't have to walk Suzy any more after they returned from the test barn.

"She cooled out in five minutes, like she never even ran," he said.

He was silent for most of the van ride home, not hanging out that side window like he usually did, instead holding on to Suzy's halter the whole trip, studying her as if he could divine an answer to the non-performance by staring into her big brown eyes.

"He said she didn't even try," said Ham.

"Sometimes everything is about your perspective and your expectations," said Willie, "perspective" being a very big word for somebody who usually didn't use them.

"What I'm saying, 'the jockey jumps on and off and tells what he knows from sitting on their back for ten minutes, then he changes his silks and gets on another one. You 'look at it from being with them day and night. 'Both got the same expectations but you got different perspective."

Back at Hialeah they watched Suzy prance down the ramp off the van and stroll back to the barn like she hadn't a care in the world. Ham asked Willie to feel her legs in case there was something there he was missing but he said they were cold and tight.

"Remember what I told you about them mares' when they be 'horsing?" said Willie and Ham nodded that he did.

He was watching Suzie's Song pick at the flake of alfalfa he'd tossed in a corner of her stall when Willie said we haven't been out to eat since the grey mare won, so let's get Easy and go have us some of that fine Cuban food and Ham said sure I guess so.

Plenty of people who weren't home having turkey had lined up at the restaurant and Ham smiled back at the dark haired girl when she seated them right away at the table in the back where the owner usually ate.

She asked Ham where he was from and when he said Vermont, she said she'd never been that far north but she heard it was beautiful and she laughed when he said then we're even because I've never been to Cuba, but if all the girls there are as pretty as you, I'd sure like to go and the old men cooed.

"Smooth, eh?" said Willie.

"Just like Desi Arnaz," said Easy, and they both winked at the boy, tickled to see him over being upset about the race and flirting with her.

The dark haired girl's name was Carla and she sat down with them after dinner and shared some of the flan they always had for desert with their Café Cubano and as they left she slipped Ham her phone number.

Easy teased him all the way back to the track, telling him that if they went on a date that her grandmother would have to come with them since that's the way the Cubans do it, but Willie just smiled, happy that the kid had finally come out of his shell.

The next morning Ham held Suzie's Song as the veterinarian examined her and he told him that Willie was right, she'd been in heat and that would account for her poor performance in the stakes race.

"Got a follicle the size of a golf ball," he said, removing the plastic sleeve from his arm and he asked Ham if he knew what a follicle was but Ham had gotten an A in biology so he had no problem understanding what the vet was describing and told him so.

"We're always looking for assistants, so keep it in mind," said the vet and that gave Ham something to think about for the next few days and when he told Willie about the conversation Willie told him he'd make a damn good vet if that was what he wanted or anything else he decided to put his mind to for that matter.

Mister Evans didn't come to the barn until after the eight o'clock break when the maintenance crew harrowed the track and he spent most of the morning in his office, talking with Bogie. Everyone who passed the closed door could hear them inside, their voices a dull unceasing staccato.

Ham asked Willie what he thought was wrong but Willie didn't have an answer except he thought the boss was under the weather, maybe he had caught a flu up north and had not yet recovered.

When the door finally did open, Willie had to summon courage to tell the trainer that he thought Momma's Boy was done, sore all over and not really anything he could do about the arthritis and all the wear and tear that an old gelding turning ten would have after seventy-two starts.

Evans told Willie he'd respect his judgement and keep Momma's Boy around as a second stable pony since they'd be able to give him a proper dose of bute for that kind of work which they couldn't if he was running races.

Willie choked up and said he'd be happy to keep taking care of him as well as his three race horses for no extra money and Evans liked that just fine and said he'd bring Willie another horse off the farm on the next van coming their way.

As the sun began to set later and later in the evening, if they didn't go to shoot hoops or out for supper they took to sitting outside the barn with the transistor radio and they'd listen to music on a Cuban channel while they talked. Ham asked Willie if he'd ever thought about getting married and Willie said sure, he'd been married for a while but it didn't work out.

"Got a lovely daughter out of it, though. Made all the rest worth the pain and sorrow even if it didn't seem like it was at the time," said Willie.

And Ham asked a couple more questions about Willie's daughter and he said her name was Mariah and she went to college and got herself a master's degree in fine arts and he pronounced what she did as "co-ree-ographer," and that she "made up the dances" for Hollywood stars and then he changed the topic and Ham got the feeling that was all he was going to say on the subject.

The stable area was silent most nights, except maybe Saturday when a few of the stable help might get a bit rowdy as they came in late from roaming the clubs and bars but it was rare you'd see a police car inside the gates.

Easy started his night watch at eight each evening, patrolling up and down the shedrow, peeking in on the horses to make sure they had water and most of his time was spent on an old beat-up armchair outside the trainer's office, sipping the strong Cuban coffee that helped him stay awake.

He was a gentle soul who enjoyed the quiet of the barn at night and he liked to read a book as he surveyed the shedrow and occasionally he wandered out to gaze up at the splash of stars across the winter sky like he did when he was a boy in Havana.

So it was quite an event on that night in the middle of the week when Willie and Ham nearly fell out of their beds, so loud was the commotion and so close by that the walls were shaking like an earthquake when the cops weren't shy about how they rousted the occupants of the other tack room at their end of the barn.

Ham threw on his jeans and stepped out into the shedrow only to have a Hialeah policeman point a nightstick in his face and tell him to get back in his room and keep the door shut, and it seemed just that quick it was all over and they were gone.

"What happened?" Willie asked Easy, who said he'd been shocked to see the patrol car pull almost into the barn and that the cop had told him also to get lost as they staged their raid, kicking the door off its hinges and emptying the tack room, which was now sealed with yellow crime scene tape.

"Cocaina," said Easy.

He said he knew the two grooms who lived there and they didn't work for Evans but he wasn't sure who else the cops took away, just that none of their people were in trouble and it's a damn shame when drugs get in the barn.

It was dawn when Jacinto Vasquez parked his Jaguar at the end of the barn and strolled into Mister Evans' office.

Willie already had Mighty tacked up and was walking him in the shedrow when Bogie gave the jock a leg up and said they were going to go out through the paddock for a change.

The big bay colt was on his toes so much that he did a little buck-jump as he bounced out of the barn and Vasquez laughed, yelling out yee-hah as Willie handed them off to Bogie on Chester the pony and Willie and Evans followed behind on the horse path.

When they came back the jockey was telling jokes and the three old men were laughing like little kids and Mighty was prancing like a show horse.

Willie told Ham that the boss said his big colt was ready to roll and they'd be entering him for the next Saturday coming and pull out your betting cash kid, 'cause now is when you get your Christmas money.

Over the next three weeks they made half-a-dozen trips to Tropical but Mister Evans only showed up once and Bogie saddled all the horses.

Ham ran Starlight twice and she finished third both times as favorite and made it a certainty that she was going to be a five year-old maiden. And Avalanche looked like she couldn't lose on paper but she stumbled coming out of the gate and got beat a dirty nose in an allowance race.

Willie wasn't disheartened by Delilah finishing fifth in a stakes race, which was about what he expected, saying that the little track's turns were too sharp for her but it was a perfect tune-up for Hialeah where she always ran well, and when Carlos went home to Argentina Willie took his place running Carlos' old claimer who surprised them all when he won.

But it was their last runner of the year that had everyone in the barn pumped up. Mighty drew the rail with a full field of maidens on Christmas Eve, and Willie was okay with it when the boss told him he wasn't going to put blinkers on for the first out, that the colt was too good to start his career that way and it wasn't about the bet, it was about the horse.

Willie told Ham that was the Old School way of training, to let your horse develop and not rush him, so as he'd learn to pace himself and use his energy right and not get speed crazy and besides, that big colt was good enough to win anyway.

Mighty broke a beat slow and spotted most of the field a couple of lengths but he looped the bunch of them turning for home and as Vasquez dismounted he said that he hadn't sat on a better horse all year or maybe ever for that matter.

Ham had one of his recurring episodes in the winner's circle like he was looking down on the group, unable to hear their words as he floated above.

And Willie was right, they all got their Christmas money at five-to-one just because the leading trainer named Winick who flew to the track in a helicopter had a good-thing in the race and nobody ever thought he could lose, but he did that day.

After a dozen times of going to dinner at the Cuban place, Ham finally mustered some nerve and asked Carla if she'd like to go to the movies on Saturday night and he breathed a sigh of relief when she said yes and didn't say she had to bring her grandmother.

He wore his best jeans and his red shirt and might have spent half an hour before he left the barn making sure the part on his hair was straight. When he knocked on her door she asked him in to meet her family and the first thing he noticed was the tortoise shell clip she wore to hold back her long hair.

She told Ham her favorite actor was Robert Redford and there he was in a movie about a jewel robbery playing at the little yellow stucco-walled theatre in Miami Springs close to where she lived and after they took in the early show, they walked across the foot bridge over the canal to the ice cream place.

It was a warm evening and they sat at a little table on the sidewalk and talked and Ham was surprised when she said she'd never been to the race track, since she lived so close and knew so many track people from the restaurant.

And even though she never did tell him how old she was, he figured she had to be at least eighteen, being halfway through her freshman year at the Junior College and he knew she was probably thinking he was too, being a full-time working man and he was glad she didn't ask so he wouldn't have to lie.

They held hands on the way to the house and he made sure to have her home by ten o'clock like her mother said and was glad he had listened to Easy who'd told him if he was a smart guy he'd bring some candy, not for Carla but for her mother and her Abuela which was what she called her grandma.

The mile Ham had to walk back to Hialeah that night seemed like it took two minutes and he was glad Willie was awake so he could tell him what a great time they had and about the tortoise shell clip Carla wore and did you ever notice that her eyes were so dark, they were the color of that coffee that you and Easy like to drink.

Ham got a hunger pang one morning and when his last horse went out to the track he hustled over to the track kitchen to grab a fried egg sandwich to take back to the barn and he saw the red Camaro parked outside.

Spider and the older man were at a corner table having coffee with a couple of guys who might have been grooms, one that had shoulders like he lifted a lot of weights and the other that looked badly in need of a shave.

Spider was wearing a helmet and boots, as if he had been getting on horses and the older man perhaps could have been taken for a retired jockey himself if the expensive looking suit and tie he had on didn't paint him as more of a businessman, like a banker on his way to the office.

"Hey," said Ham as he passed, heading for the exit.

"Hey," said Spider, barely looking up.

Ham was halfway out the door when he heard Spider call his name.

"Greer, wait," he said, following Ham out onto the steps with his whip in hand.

"Here, give me a call, I need to talk," said Spider, proffering a slip of paper and just as quickly he turned on his heel, back into the track kitchen.

Ham glanced at the childish scrawl and stuffed the phone number in his pocket as he hurried back to the barn, wondering why Spider would want to talk with him, having had plenty of chances before when he never said more than a few words.

Later he told Willie what had happened and Willie told him I'd stay away from that kid if I were you, he's probably up to no good.

It was the week after Christmas, late in the morning when all the barn work was done and Bogie told everyone that Mister Evans wanted them to come to end of the shedrow outside his office and when they were all there the trainer stood in the doorway and said he was having heart problems and was going to have to retire right away.

Some of the grooms had been with him for over twenty years, and Jake had been his foreman for five and they all turned somber, dulled by the thought of losing such a kind man who'd been their leader for so long and a couple of them began to cry.

"I've asked Bogie to take over for the time being and hopefully most of the owners will stick with him and keep the stable together. My Mary's getting married in the spring and moving to Aiken, so I guess this is good-bye," he said, and he started to pass out envelopes and embrace each of them as he did.

Ham and Willie walked to the track kitchen in silence as each contemplated the consequences of Evans' words. They took their trays to a corner table and before Ham tasted his lunch he asked:

"What do you think we should do?"

Willie had that furrow back in his brow, the one that once seemed permanent but that Ham hadn't seen in quite a while.

"Dunno," said Willie, "I was planning to stay with Mister Evans the rest of my days. Ain't many racetrackers 'get to retire, they usually stay at doing what they do until they drop over one day in the barn. Must be pretty serious for him to just 'up and quit like this."

"What about Bogie?" said Ham, but he knew Bogie was already half retired himself, keeping to Florida all year round to be near his kids and grandkids and wasn't likely to be going on with a stable that needed to move north in the spring.

"You got to do a lot of things in life before you find yourself, son, and some folks never do. Follow that Golden Rule and you won't go wrong, doing to others like you'd have them do for you. And don't worry when things don't work out the way you think they should. Maybe you just weren't thinking right," said Willie.

Ham didn't grow up religious and he sure didn't appreciate sermons but he never felt like Willie was preaching to him, just putting what he believed into his advice.

"Might only be the Good Lord's way of telling us to do something else. 'Depends on my big horse, if I still have him. Maybe I'll head back home to Kentucky when winter's over, and you can go back to school," said Willie.

CHAPTER 6

So Hialeah seemed like a paradise to Hamilton Greer, the kid who'd grown up below the granite crags of the Green Mountains and who now found himself looking up at a palm tree filled with squawking wild parrots. Instead of pine-covered mountains, it seemed there were palm trees everywhere he looked.

Royal palms lined the roadway into the track, tall and straight as Doric columns, and there were coconut palms and foxtail palms, date palms and pygmy palms scattered about the grounds. Along with the bougainvillea and jasmine blossoms that framed the stands as well as the orange and lemon and banana trees that you could pick the fruit right off and nobody cared.

And every day there were horses... the finest horses a man could hope to see.

The epicenter of the equine world in winter was at Hialeah and in the months of January and February when football fever abated, horses again took over the newspaper sports section, and if President Nixon hadn't been talking about the conflict ending soon in Viet Nam, Secretariat might well have been on the front page.

Willie cast a cynic's eye on the politics of war:

"'Greatest scourge of mankind,' that's what Thomas Jefferson called it."

Secretariat won the Horse of the Year title hands down and he was certain to be the overwhelming favorite for the Kentucky Derby, lots of believers hoping for a Triple Crown Winner. It had been over twenty years since Arcaro booted home Citation in the red and blue Calumet silks, and they were ready for another hero.

And of course the non-believers said Big Red's breeding wasn't right for him to get the longer distances of the Classics, but Willie said those folks are going to get re-educated for sure and they'll all change their tune by the time that colt crosses the finish line next June in the Belmont Stakes.

But Secretariat wasn't going to run in Florida at all in the winter of 1973, trainer Laurin already on record that he'd make his first start in March in the Bay Shore at Aqueduct, then go in the Wood Memorial, so the winter focus fell on those other three year old colts who might be up against him later in the spring, the horses that would prep in the Bahamas and the Everglades and Flamingo Stakes at Hialeah or later at Gulfstream Park in March when they honed up in the Hutcheson and the Florida Derby.

Each of those races were worth serious money, with every eye on the prize in Louisville for the first Saturday in May, yet all still knowing that a lot of things have to happen just right for you before you even get in the gate for that big one.

The Evans barn, which was now actually the Alexander barn, still had the red and yellow wall plaques and the stone jockey outside but Bogie didn't seem to be too keen to run any of the horses, like he was waiting for something to happen and most got moved to other trainers before he got a chance to run them anyway.

Bogie kept training the horses the same way he always did, but Ham came to understand what Willie meant when he said some guys make great assistants, but not great trainers.

"A lot of what the trainer does is more about training the owners than it is training the horses. Horses can 'about train themselves if you keep 'em happy. And owners can get to thinking they know more than you do really fast but the truth is they aren't happy unless they 'winnin," said Willie.

Their barn was last in the row of barns and sat at the end of the stable area furthest from the action, so it was quiet and peaceful but still not that far a walk for Ham on those afternoons when he'd head over to the grandstand and blend in with the other fans.

He liked to go to the paddock to make notes on his program for each horse like a trainer getting ready to claim one and then he'd take the escalator to the second floor to a spot at the end of the free seats opposite the eighth-pole. That was where most of the action took place in any race, where the horse on the lead would either push on gamely or run out of gas when the late-runners closed in.

Sometimes Willie would go up there and sit with him and point out things Ham wouldn't have picked up on by himself, like how the riders switched their sticks or a horse getting shut off at the rail, or the one time when they stood at the outside fence and heard the faint hum when a renegade jockey used his buzzer.

"He's pluggin' that one in," said Willie, and he explained to Ham that as long as money was involved there would always be cheaters in the game, and anyone who'd been around as long as he had knew who they were and avoided them as much as possible.

"Lay down with dogs, 'you're gonna get fleas," said Willie.

It was almost sunset and Willie and Ham were on the way back from shooting some baskets when a car with blacked-out windows raised a cloud of dust as it pulled away from their barn, heading toward the stable exit.

"Somebody's in a hurry," said Willie.

When they got to the barn they went right to their tackroom and the door was still locked but the door to the room at the other side of the barn was open wide.

They looked inside and the cots were askew and there was wood paneling that someone had ripped off the walls scattered all over the place.

"Looking for something," said Willie, "I hope they found it."

On a quiet weekday, Carla came to the races with her brothers Raul and Fausto, who were nice enough, but flanked her like a pair of bodyguards wherever they went and Ham knew there wouldn't be any hand-holding that day. He got them some passes and seats through Buddy, one of the clerks in the racing office and he wore a new shirt with his best jeans when he showed them around.

Willie was running Delilah in the feature and he told Ham that Toady could carry the bucket and to go on and bring that pretty girl and her brothers to the paddock, 'cause the man who owns Delilah loves to have a lot of attention and shake a lot of hands.

The brothers had some beginner's luck picking a couple of winners, but Carla was more taken with the beauty of the place; the park-like grounds, the aquarium full of tropical fish and of course, the flamingos.

Each day between the seventh and eighth race, someone dressed as a Seminole Indian paddled a canoe across the infield lake and the entire flock, a couple of hundred birds, would take to the air and do a couple of loops over the track as soft music played on the P.A. system.

"Ladies and gentlemen, the world famous flight of the flamingos," said the announcer.

Carla told Ham how her mother said it had been a big deal back in the days when the U.S. and Cuba got along, when the track owner arrived in Cuba to get those flamingos from Batista before Castro came in the fifties and their family fled to Miami, not trusting him and Che Guevara who they knew were communists.

They went to the paddock and when Ham introduced Carla and her brothers to Deliah's owner, he did like Willie had told him to and made the man feel good when he said that he thought she was the best horse in the barn, even if it wasn't true.

The owner had flown in just for the race and made them come and sit in a box seat with him and for luck he gave them each a two-dollar win ticket on Delilah. Willie's mare strolled out of the gate like she always did and everybody in the place could see she would have won if the jockey didn't have to take her so wide.

Even though, the man was happy enough with second and proud of having such a nice running mare and he bought drinks for all of them before he rushed off to the airport to catch an Eastern Airlines flight back to New York.

By the end of the day, each of the brothers were over a hundred dollars ahead and Raul said he thought Ham was a pretty nice guy to have invited them and maybe they'd let him hang around their little sister for a while longer.

It was noontime on a dark day meaning there weren't any races so the barn was very quiet when the black Crown Victoria parked at the end of the barn. Two big guys in dark suits walked into the shedrow and started looking in every stall until the taller of the two tried to pet one of the maiden colts and it took a bite at him, ripping the shoulder of his jacket.

Ham spotted them from the other end of the barn and hurried to head them off before they had any more misfortunes.

"Can I help you?" said Ham.

"'The boss here?" said the detective with the torn jacket, flashing a badge.

"Mister Alexander will be back at feed time, about three o'clock," said Ham and the other man took out a pad and a ballpoint pen.

"And you are?"

"Hamilton Greer, sir."

"What do you do, Hamilton?"

"Groom, sir, I'm a groom."

They asked Ham if he was in the barn the night of the raid and a lot of questions he wasn't sure how to answer but when they finished one of them gave him a business card that said Dade County Public Safety Department and told him to call if he thought of anything else.

After the detectives left he wondered why they had come to their side of the barn when the room they had raided was on the other side, and another trainer's grooms the ones that got taken away that night. The whole outfit had disappeared the day after the raid but the stalls had all been filled by the end of the week and until now Ham hadn't given the event another thought.

He told Willie what happened and Willie said just give that card to Bogie and hope you never see those guys again.

Mighty's win first time out attracted plenty of attention and every day someone new would come by the barn, asking was the trainer there and if that big bay colt might be for sale. Bogie liked to tell them they had to come back when Mister Evans was there, making them spin their wheels, since he wasn't the least interested in having a horse like that leave his barn.

Willie said they were bloodstock agents, guys who sold horses for a living and took a commission or percentage of the price and he sure hoped he got to run that colt a few times before he got snatched away for big money.

Willie was putting the tack on Mighty just as the sun came up on a Saturday morning when Bogie and a bent-over old man with a cane came to the stall door.

"There he is Mister Russo," said Bogie.

"That's my baby," said the old man and Willie held Mighty by his halter, squared him up to face the man.

"Pretty good, is he Willie?" said Mister Russo.

"Best these hands ever touched, boss," said Willie.

"How many years 'you been rubbing my horses, Willie?"

"I think Mister Eisenhower was President," said Willie, and the man laughed.

"You think I should sell him?"

"You should if you thinks you can get a better one," said Willie.

Willie and Russo followed on the horse path as Ivan rode Mighty next to Bogie on the pony, heading toward the paddock. When horse and rider went through the tunnel to the track, the two men stopped to admire the bronze statue of Citation that stood in the middle of a pool with hundreds of goldfish swimming among the lily pads.

"A man offered me a quarter of a million dollars for that colt, Willie," said Mister Russo.

"That would be a considerable sum," said Willie.

"Know what happened when the two fools met?" said the old man.

"The one that offered too much and the other one that turned him down?" said Willie.

"Count me one of them fools," said the old man,

"I waited too long for a good one and I'm too old to spend the money anyway. Plus my old friend Willie would never speak to me again."

A month had passed since Suzie's Song ran in the stake at Tropical, and she'd had a couple of stiff works in the interim so it seemed logical that Bogie might be getting ready to put her in again. Ham studied the condition book and guessed an allowance race going five furlongs might be one she could win but when he picked up the Saturday entries, there she was, back in a stakes race going seven.

"Dang," said Ham, "Looks like some killers in there."

"Your girl's the one who's the wolf in sheep-clothes," was all Willie said.

This time there was barely a mention of Suzie in the *Morning Telegraph*, and all those smart horse-pickers that made her best bet of the day last time didn't give her a chance, since this race was longer and she'd shown nothing last time.

"Trouble with that thing," said Willie, pointing at Ham's *Morning Telegraph*, "It tells you where they been, but it don't tell you where they be goin'."

Ham managed an insincere laugh, but he wasn't about to get overconfident like last time, especially since Suzie had been training just as well then as she was now and she never ran a step and besides, she was going to have a new jockey since Fires' agent had spun them to ride another horse in the race that just happened to be the favorite.

There was a huge crowd at Hialeah that Saturday, mostly there to see the horses in the Everglades Stakes, lined up to try and make it to the Kentucky Derby.

Jimmy Croll trained a colt called Royal and Regal and he looked like a cinch to win it since he'd taken the Bahamas Stakes at seven furlongs, and he'd even put another horse in as part of an entry, which was that "rabbit" Willie talked about to keep the pace honest.

Ham and Willie had Suzie's Song on the horse path to the paddock well before the announcement came over the P.A. calling for the horses in the seventh race.

Willie showed Ham how to stall a little when they walked her around the ring and let her pick at the grass, and when Bogie put the saddle on, she was so relaxed that she barely turned a hair.

Mike Manganello had won a Kentucky Derby a few years before and he was the leading rider up at Tampa but the purses were a little light there and the one here was twenty thousand, making it worth the road trip even if he finished in the top three.

"Good luck," said Ham to the jockey as he handed Suzie off to the pony boy, but Manganello didn't answer, so stone-faced was he and so absorbed into his task at hand.

The race began in the seven furlong chute in a grove carved out of those tall Australian pines and this time Suzie flew from her outside post, clearing the field as soon as they made their way onto the main track.

The jockey took a long hold and let the filly make her own pace as she kept a few lengths between her and the second horse all the way to the top of the stretch before the late runners came after her.

Fires had the favorite Lazy Belle in a drive and she was making up ground with every stride as the announcer's voice rang in Ham's ears, and he once again sensed himself floating above the crowd and looking down as the sounds beginning to echo:

"Suzie's Song--- Lazy Belle--- Lazy Belle--- Suzie's Song---"

The "PHOTO" sign was on and the wait seemed to take an eternity and a half, with Ham and Willie and the favorite's groom and hot walker all there on the track as the two horses circled, none of them knowing who'd get to go in and have their picture taken, until the board went dark for a moment and the numbers lit up...

"DEAD HEAT" it said, Suzie's number beneath Lazy Belle's, only because it was a higher number. Willie laughed and told Ham that was one he had on him now, never having a dead heat in fifty years on the track.

"What do they do about the money?" asked Ham.

"Add first and second together and split it down the middle," said Willie with a wink, "Better than getting beat a nose."

Mid-week and Ham was in his spot in the grandstand and the words in the *Morning Telegraph* seemed to make as much sense as those carved on the Rosetta Stone when a woman behind him cleared her throat.

"Hello, darlin," she said.

He knew it was Lizzie but her long blonde hair was dark now and cropped and she hid her face under a big floppy straw hat like one of the tourists.

"Call me Shirley," she said with exactly what a person from England might imagine was a Brooklyn accent.

There wasn't another horseplayer within fifty yards, so she slipped off her sunglasses and moved to the seat next to him.

"I thought you got deported," said Ham and she told him the story of how she was sent to Canada and supposed to go home to England but managed to slip back through Vermont and how she'd thought of him when she did.

She said she'd had an ex-husband back in London who liked to drink too much and knock her around and there'd be icicles on these palm trees before they got her to go back.

"There's plenty of us 'illegals around here," she said and she told him she hoped to get on some horses at Gulfstream, knowing a couple of the trainers there were Brits and friends from a while back and she'd get by.

Lizzie gave him a match book with her phone number written in it and said to call sometime and they'd have a meal and she still hadn't forgotten that he brought her flowers in the hospital and before she left she gave him a kiss square on the mouth and shortly thereafter he gave up trying to read the paper.

The next two times when Mighty had his workouts Mister Russo came out to watch, and he and Bogie decided they'd run the colt the following week if the race filled, for non-winners of two races at seven furlongs.

"Take a monster to beat him," said Willie and Ham knew that was serious talk for a guy who never bragged.

The race did fill and Mighty won in hand that Saturday, Vasquez taking the big bay back to last in a full field and letting him get some education and a little dirt in his face, since the races were only going to get tougher from here on.

And old man Russo hopped down to the winners circle like he didn't need that cane at all and said he'd take the trophy home to Chicago with him and be back in a couple of weeks if Mighty was running in a stakes race and that Big Red had better watch out now.

They were at the Cuban place, just Ham and Willie in early for their usual celebration dinner, and it was a slow night but Carla was off, so they took their time and talked a bit while Willie sipped his coffee, in no hurry to get back to the barn.

Ham asked Willie what he thought they should do in a couple of months when the stable broke up, seeing as there was no chance of Bogie leaving Florida and most of the horses they rubbed belonged to owners from up north, so they had to go.

"I'll stay with my big horse, 'long as I can keep the job," said Willie, "and so will Bogie, don't kid yourself. A good horse is hard to come by."

Ham told him that the vet was asking did he want a job and maybe that would be a good idea, what did Willie think and the old man didn't take a second but said:

"Race track is a good life if it suits you, and some ways' it's like the circus... 'got its own animals and jugglers and clowns. You just keep moving on, doing the same thing a different way. But sometimes it's okay to go away for a while 'cause it is a place 'you can always come back to."

Ham walked Avalanche out to the quarter pole gap for her last breeze before she'd run on the weekend and Ivan jogged her off the wrong way to back up to the half-mile pole. Bogie liked to have his horses warm up a little before a workout and Ham could see him in the distance, up in the stands with his binoculars trained on the grey mare.

Ham was leaning on the outside fence when Spider passed, galloping a grand looking chestnut and he noticed the older man there too, a stopwatch in his hand.

The man nodded and when he moved in Ham's direction he had a bit of a limp.

"You're a friend of Kevin's," he said.

Ham told him he didn't know anybody named Kevin and the man said maybe you know him as Spider, that's what he's been calling himself since he started hanging around the track and Ham said oh yeah, Spider.

"He told me you ran away too," said the man and he introduced himself as Arlen Quinn and said he'd been a jockey but he'd gotten hurt in a bad spill and didn't want to chance his only son to the same fate and that's what they'd fallen out over.

First it was bickering, then fighting more and more after Spider's mother fell ill and died until the boy had taken off, gone for over a year before he came back and they patched things up.

"Sometimes fathers and sons need to bang heads," he said.

And he said Spider had ridden won a few races at the bush tracks in Louisiana where they didn't have many rules but they sure could horseback and he'd decided to get a stable together and help his kid with his dream instead of battle with him. They were going to assemble a string of horses that they could run in New York and Spider would ride them all.

"He looks good on a horse," said Ham.

"He's been around them since he was two," said Mister Quinn.

Spider had his horse at a walk on the outside fence as he approached them and when his father turned away, he held his hand to his face, thumb and little finger spread, signaling Ham to "call me."

Ham couldn't wait to tell Willie about Spider and his father and how his father had been a jockey too and maybe the little guy really was going to be one since he was bred for it. He thought maybe Spider had straightened out and when he looked for the paper with Spider's phone number he couldn't find it and figured he must have lost it.

And he told Willie how Spider's father had quit riding after he took a bad fall and how he had started a horse transportation company that shipped racehorses all over the world, buying a lot of them in South America and re-selling them to rich Americans. Ham said that Spider's old man had a couple dozen horses in his stable already and they were going to race at the east coast tracks and the little guy was going to ride them all.

Willie seemed surprised and just said "huh, is that right?"

CHAPTER 7

When the racing meet ended and the action moved about twenty miles away to Gulfstream Park, Bogie still kept the horses at Hialeah and would ship them over when they had a race and as more and more outfits shipped out the place got quiet as a church.

Ham started walking around the track on the afternoons that he didn't have a horse to run, just to burn off some of his restless energy... of which he had an endless supply.

It seemed like he was always at the barn, first person up in the morning to have one of those strong, sweet little Cuban coffees that Easy made and he was the last to finish work in the afternoon, although in fact he never did actually leave.

If he wasn't in the shedrow raking or cleaning or in the stalls with his horses or helping the vet or the blacksmith or the horse dentist, he was likely in the tack room he shared with Willie, reading a book or studying the

Morning Telegraph or listening to the radio, but he was still there.

Ham read more and more and not just the racing pages and the *Ainsle's Guide to Thoroughbred Racing* that Willie had given him, saying it was the bible of those serious about studying the "art" of horse handicapping, and he'd nearly committed that volume to memory.

He found a leather-bound copy of Chaucer's *Canterbury Tales* in a second-hand shop and a dusty edition of *Hamlet* and daydreamed of the English countryside. When he said he'd like to someday visit Stratford-on-Avon, Willie teased him that he'd probably had both books in school and never cracked either, but now he was quoting the Bard.

So the walks, which eventually turned into jogs and finally into long distance runs were the only time Ham left the barn area during the day, save the rare trip that he and Willie took to the Seaquarium or Parrot Jungle or the Serpentarium or if he went to downtown Miami or Calle Ocho with Carla when she wanted to shop.

Most evenings when he hung out with Willie they shot hoops until it got too dark or if Carla wasn't working, he'd take her to a movie and twice they went to a concert at her college.

One night she asked him if he had I.D. so they could go to a bar and have a drink and dance. She knew his birthday was the seventeenth of August but she never asked what year and he lied and told her he'd had an I.D. but he'd lost it and she said her brother knew someone who'd get him another one.

Willie was the only person who actually knew how old Ham was since he was the one who'd taken him to get his track license, but because he was a taller than average kid and mature for his age and one who would get a five o'clock shadow real quick, no one else suspected he was still only sixteen.

Occasionally his thoughts would drift to Vermont, not exactly reminiscing but musing on the past versus the present and trying to figure out where he might be heading in the future, thinking about those he'd known back there and what might have become of them. The ski resorts were the mainstay of his hometown, and more than likely the majority of his classmates would never leave, signing on for a lifetime of toil on the slopes.

The day Ham hit the road he swore he'd never return but as time passed began to think he might recant after he'd had some accomplishments and he could go back to Manchester as a man of the world, not just the police chief's kid who ran away.

Back in high school other guys would ask him to go across the border to New York where the legal age was eighteen and he'd buy the beer for a party because some places there wouldn't check I.D and it was easy enough for him to pass for legal.

But Hamilton had seen his dad drink a lot, seen how the man would change so much, how he turned angry and argued endlessly with his mother and he thought it might be the liquor. Ham drank as much as anyone at parties but his hangovers were brutal so he stayed away from it otherwise.

In high school he had a girlfriend named Diana that he called "Moonbeam" who lived with her single mom. She wore tie-dyed clothes and her blonde hair in long braids and he wore bell-bottom jeans and chambray work shirts and Frye boots.

They kept to themselves and didn't bother much with the preppies or the jocks or even go to the junior prom and gravitated to the folk singers like Dylan and Guthrie and Seeger and once even went to see Peter, Paul and Mary in a concert at the college in Middlebury.

But when his mother started to bug him about reading the beats instead of his school assignments, Ham just sought them out more and he and Diana talked about hitch hiking across the country to San Francisco. She was a year older than Ham and after her graduation they had an argument and when she took off to follow the Grateful Dead it was only about a month or so until he hit the road himself.

After his parents' divorce Ham felt that he and his mom were pretty close until she met a guy named Steve and all of a sudden she decided Hamilton had to shape up. Steve was from Manchester as well and he'd been a Ranger in Viet Nam, pretty rough duty for a guy who said he started out wanting to be a teacher or a social worker.

When Steve got out of the service he'd headed home to the Green Mountains and when they met at a church social, Ham's mom was enchanted to find a person she liked who had so much in common, each feeling deserted and left with kids to raise on their own.

She kidded that it was going to be like *The Brady Bunch*, and how funny it was that Hamilton would be the only boy with four girls to deal with.

And the girls did get along pretty well for teen-agers, leaving the rebellion to their brother and him the one castigated while they took joy in emulating their TV counterparts.

When Ham felt the walls closing in he'd go out behind the old barn and smoke a little pot with Anna who was Steve's oldest daughter and the only one he felt the least bit close with.

Anna said she was going to go to Castelton State and study Political Science and Ham was right, the people running things didn't know what the hell they were doing and maybe someday she'd get herself elected president and straighten this country out.

Ham went to a few parties with Carla and when they danced and he held her in his arms and smelled her hair and the nape of her neck it was lucky for him she didn't have a wild streak or he'd have been in trouble, sure to do anything she wanted him to.

One night after the movies they stopped in the middle of the footbridge over the canal to have a look at some water birds that were diving after a school of mullet, the sides of the fish flashing silver when the moonlight hit them as they turned this way and that.

He had his arm around her shoulder and she turned to face him with her eyes closed and they kissed and he was almost dizzy, overcome with the sweetness of her breath and the softness of her hair brushing his face.

Willie teased him the next day when he kept dropping things and once when he walked out of Starlight's stall without snapping the cross-tie, it was a good thing the mare didn't follow him right out into the shedrow.

If they didn't have plans to see each other, Ham called Carla three or four times a day from the pay phone by the kitchen, using change from a Mason jar he kept on the shelf in the tack room and he used his pocket knife to carve her initials with his inside a heart on the big Australian pine outside the barn. And he didn't care if anyone teased him about it and for a while he considered having her name tattooed on his arm but that never happened.

At one of the parties someone passed a joint around and Carla took a toke and handed it to him. He pretty much faked his inhale, afraid he'd get loaded and do something stupid, and it was a good thing he didn't get high that night because later in the evening she told him that she had been accepted at a college in California, and she'd be moving soon and how much she was going to miss him.

It took his breath away hearing that, and Ham did his best to act cool, wishing her luck and saying how much he'd miss her but inside he was crushed because somehow deep inside he might have thought that they'd be together forever.

Those walks that had turned into runs gave Ham plenty of time to think about what it was he wanted to do, not necessarily with his life, which was too big a question right then, but at least what he'd do after the Florida season ended. He had been seriously considering that he might stay and find a job at Calder just because of Carla, but now that she was leaving he just wanted to move on.

After he said his good-byes, Mister Evans had shipped Chester to his daughter in South Carolina, so most of the horses still in their barn belonged to Mister Russo; Mighty and the three maidens that he had bred that had yet to race and Willie rubbed all of those.

Ham still had Starlight, but Suzie and Avalanche were gone, moved by their owners to the big name trainers and he still had Passport, the cheap claimer that Carlos left behind when he packed it in and went home to Argentina.

His other two were geldings that belonged to Bogie and his son the lawyer from Miami and those were sure to stay at Calder for the summer so the son could bring his kids out on Saturday mornings to feed them carrots with their grandpa.

Ham and Willie took the shuttle van to Gulfstream a couple of times a week to run horses, but Hialeah was starting to get a little too quiet for Ham and some of the outfits had shipped out already and he knew everyone was going to scatter in less than a month.

At least when the races were right there he could walk over and watch from his spot high in the grandstand, but with no racing there it felt like a ghost town and besides, it was getting warmer as spring approached and the afternoons began to drag.

One night Ham was weighing his options:

"How many years do you have to go to school to be a vet," he said.

"Is that what you want to do?" said Willie.

And Ham told him he didn't know if he should keep rubbing horses or do something else, but the one thing he was pretty sure of was that he wanted to stay around the track, make that his life, and Willie seemed pleased at that, saying:

"You can look at things 'simple or you can make everything complicated. But simple is easier and you'll sleep better. Wait 'til we get back to Saratoga and then decide what's next. Maybe you'll want to keep rubbing horses or maybe be a trainer or a vet or maybe even go home to your momma, but that's probably not what you'll do."

Every year after the end of the meet Hialeah had an auction of young horses, two year olds that were already saddle broke and trained and could be ready to run by the late spring or early summer.

The sales arena was on the other side of the track from the barn area and no one ever went back there until about a week or so before the sale when consignors began to bring their horses in to gallop over the track and they began to show them to the bloodstock agents and prospective buyers.

One morning Doc Barnett was going over Starlight to try and figure out why she had run so poorly the day before at Gulfstream and he mentioned the sales to Ham.

"We could use some help over there if you want to make a few extra bucks," he said.

"Sounds good," said Ham and Willie told him good for you, boy, learn something new and you never know what can come of it.

The sales grounds were bustling and the vet taught Ham the fundamentals of horse-trading, how the sales agents would shine up their stock and the little tricks they used to make their horses look as good as they possibly could, since after all, they were trying to sell them. He showed Ham how the clever outfits knew all the ways to take an edge, like rubbing a little oil on those young colts and fillies that had been training up north in Virginia and Kentucky and had to be clipped of their winter coats.

And how they touched up their feet with polish and the way they taught those horses to behave on the walking ring when the buyers studied them going back and forth and how the best sellers used savvy riders in the morning, making them gallop along with their necks bowed and how the few who did breeze would wear blinkers to keep their mind on business.

"Line him up and make sure his head isn't down, and those hind legs, get them lined up too," said the vet,

"A good showman can't make a crooked one straight, but a bad showman can sure make a straight one look crooked."

They went from barn to barn, taking care of horses that might be sore from shipping or from so much moving in and out of their stalls but most of the consignors were Doc Barnett's clients from previous years, and he did what he could to make the iffy ones sound with a shot of bute if they were a little "off" or some penicillin if they had the snots.

The auction took place on Monday and Tuesday nights, on the days that there was no racing at Gulfstream and it started in the evening and felt more like a party than a horse sale which was how Doc said the people running the show wanted it to seem, getting them what he called "lubricated" with free drinks.

Well dressed people holding cocktails wandered outside the arena where the horses were assembled before they went in to get auctioned off, the women glamorous in evening dresses and lots of jewelry, and some of the men even in tuxedos but nearly all of them in jacket and tie and the chauffeurs lined up their limousines at the entrance to the arena.

When Doc told him he was done for the day, Ham wandered around the grounds, watching the trainers as they tried to convince their owners to spend amounts that Ham couldn't conceive of, buying horses that had yet to run.

Willie told him that's just another way of gambling, and those people either have a lot of money they got doing something else or they're using somebody else's money to buy those horses.

Either way, he said, it's like shooting craps with a horse until you put them in the gate for a race and find out if they can really run. He figured Mighty was worth more than any of those unraced two year olds and said again how he hoped Mister Russo would resist the temptation to sell.

The first sales horse would go through the ring at seven in the evening and on the second night Ham brought along a catalog the vet gave him and found himself an out of the way spot at the back of the room where he could get a good view of both the horses and the folks who were doing the bidding.

The horses were led into the arena by their grooms and handed off to a handler in the roped-off area in front of the auctioneer's podium who got them to stand straight while the bid-spotters shouted "Yup!" whenever anyone signaled their intent. There were a few hundred of those folks in the round building, seated as to surround the auctioneer and the small man in the ring with the horse, and down in one of the front rows Ham saw Spider and his old man and the two guys they'd been with in the track kitchen.

Ham's eyes were wide as the bids flew over one horse after another with some going for hundreds of thousands of dollars and the crowd applauded wildly after the auctioneer dropped his gavel on the highest priced ones.

When the bidding came to a halt on a smallish bay filly at ninety thousand dollars, the auctioneer pointed at the man Ham knew as Spider's father, saying:

"Sold to Arlen Quinn..." and after he signed his name they all got up and left the room. Ham read the filly's page in the sales catalog and the pedigree had plenty of that black type that Willie told him could make a racehorse valuable.

Ham and Willie took two of the horses that hadn't run yet to Gulfstream for maiden claiming races and the first one which belonged to Bogie finished dead last and the other was Mister Russo's and that finished up the track too. Bogie seemed relieved when his got claimed and went off to the racing office right away when Mister Russo's was taken, wanting to call the old man and give him the good news that he wouldn't have to pay anymore to feed a horse that was that slow.

"Down to six and a pony," said Bogie as he drove them back to Hialeah since there was no point in their riding the van with no horses and he told them he was planning to run Mighty in a stakes race and if the colt ran as well as they expected, he'd take whatever he had left to Keeneland pretty soon.

He said Willie could take care of Mighty and the two maidens belonging to Mister Russo and Ham could rub whatever was left and do the hotwalking, but he could have the title of shedrow foreman instead of any more money and they both agreed to that.

Easy came by the barn to visit that afternoon and brought some media noches, those Cuban ham and pork and Swiss cheese and pickle sandwiches that he knew they liked.

Ham and Easy set up a card table and chairs under one of the pine trees and they were ready to have a picnic when from inside the barn Mighty gave a loud cough and Willie jumped out of his seat to go and investigate and before he got there the horse did it again.

"Barking like a dog. 'Happens this time every year when they get to bringing in those babies," said Willie, "babies" meaning the early two-year olds that were arriving from the farms where they'd had their preliminary training and now were in to get cranked up for the races.

They ate their sandwiches in near silence, resigned to knowing that cough would be enough to keep Mighty on the shelf for a while.

"What 'I tell you, son? Get a good one and trouble is right around the corner. May be lucky in the end, we don't try to chase those Derby horses anyway.

Ham and Willie watched the color TV in the Hialeah rec room along with a lot of the other grooms as Secretariat took the Bay Shore Stakes at Aqueduct, everyone there knowing the Derby was only six weeks away and it was getting down to the survival of the fittest who would get to go to Kentucky.

Big Red won by four and a half lengths, running away from the other five horses on a sloppy track and once again he ducked in and had to sweat another objection but this time the result stood and Willie said that jock better be careful, leaning on the bit with a free-running horse like that, maybe he doesn't run straight 'cause he feels it too much in his mouth.

Monday morning Bogie came to the barn and right away summoned Willie and Ham to his office. His eyes welled with tears as he told them that Mister Russo had had a heart attack and passed away over the weekend and that he knew his kids wouldn't keep the horses, none of them caring about racing like their old man did, and it was a sure thing they'd be selling Mighty.

He said it had been a nice dream they had, him and Willie and Ham, of going on the road with a good horse, one that would win a lot of stakes races, but it wasn't going to happen and he was sorry for that. He said he'd keep training until all the horses were sold and he'd take care of them both with some money when he got his commission for Mighty but they should both look after themselves and find another job real soon.

Even though they were running Passport in a late race, Ham and Willie took the first van to Gulfstream so they could walk around and spread the word to let a few folks know they'd soon be looking for work. Most every trainer they spoke to already knew Willie and each of them told him he could start as soon as they had an opening but Willie made sure they all knew it was a package deal, and the kid had to come along too.

Passport went off as the favorite in a $5,000 claiming sprint and finished second and got claimed, which was what Bogie said was the next best thing that could have happened if he didn't win and when Ham and Willie went back to the receiving barn to get their things, a young girl was waiting with a note.

"My dad asked me to give this to Willie," she said, and Willie said thanks and took the note and handed it to Ham.

After the girl left, Ham read the note out loud:

"Please call me at home, I need a new assistant trainer. And bring your kid, we're going to Kentucky."

The note was signed "J.B." and there was a phone number.

Willie laughed and told Ham that J.B. was from Kansas but he raced all over the country and that he'd known him since he was a kid and that his father and grandfather had both been trainers and damn good ones too. He said they should both be going to work for that man, and that they could help Bogie until they went up to Keeneland with J.B. and then back to Belmont.

"Things always work out," said Willie.

Most of the barns at Hialeah were empty since their former occupants succumbed to the same itinerant instinct that brought them there, splitting town to head back north to the same barns they came from last fall.

"Too hot, too muggy," they said, the guys who'd broke and run south when the first frost hit back at Belmont, and with the end of Gulfstream still a few weeks away, Ham and Willie's barn was the only one left with horses in it.

When Bogie dropped them off back at Hialeah there was a little white car parked at the end of the barn. Lizzie was at the card table reading a paperback, some romance novel.

"Hello, fellas," she said.

"Hi," said Ham as she first gave him a hug, then Willie.

"You make me dizzy Miss Lizzie," said Willie and she giggled.

She'd given up the masquerade, lost the dark hair for her natural blonde.

"You still evading the long arm of the law?" said Willie.

Lizzie shook her head.

"'Got a sponsor. 'Buys me a little time to try for a green card. I was thinking maybe handsome there might want to get married and make me an honest woman.'"

Willie laughed and so did Ham but he was blushing and maybe his palms were damp as he wasn't sure if she was serious or not, the way she was looking at him. There were a couple of white paper bags on the card table.

"I brought you boys a gourmet dinner," said Lizzie and she started to unpack the Chinese food. They took their time with the egg rolls and the spare ribs and orange chicken and white rice and talked about Saratoga and it was nearly dark when Ham began to clean up.

Lizzie said she was making a living by working free-lance, but she wanted to go back to New York after Gulfstream finished, and did Willie know anyone that could use a good gallop girl.

"Sure, do you know a good one?" said Willie and she threw her fortune cookie at him.

He told her after they came back to Belmont from Keeneland she should come on up and he'd introduce her to J.B. Willie said he hadn't decided if he would take the offer of the job as assistant trainer, but he and Ham would be working for that stable for sure since the horses were good and the pay steady, and most important J.B. was a real horseman who knew what he was doing, not like these ninety-day wonders who got a trainer's license when they didn't even know how to pick out a horse's foot.

"Perfect," said Lizzie, "I can be a June bride."

She gave them each a peck on the cheek when she left and told Ham to save his money, 'cause she didn't want a puny little ring, it had better be a proper rock.

Ham and Willie caught a ride to Gulfstream and watched from the rail as Royal and Regal won the Florida Derby and Willie said he's a nice horse but that gelding Forego that finished second is the real thing and mark my words they're going to hear plenty from him before it's all over.

Waiting to catch a ride back to Hialeah on one of the shuttle vans gave them time to watch the last race and there it was on the track program, Spider's name "Kevin Quinn" with three asterisks next to it meaning he was a bug boy who hadn't yet won five races and as far as Ham and Willie knew, he might not have won any.

The horse was a six year-old South American gelding and by the charts in the *Morning Telegraph* it hadn't come close to the winner's circle in two years, so the thirty-to-one odds in the program were probably flattering.

Ham and Willie went to the paddock and watched Spider, surrounded by a heavy-set man in a white guayabera and a couple of other well-fed gents sporting linen suits. Spider nodded a lot while the trainer spoke and when the assistant gave him a leg up, the trainer lit a cigar and they could hear him say "*Suerte, Araña.*"

"Guess we're not the only ones 'calling him Spider," said Willie.

The race was a cheap claimer for non-winners of two ever at a mile and an eighth and when the horses were loading in the gate, Ham watched the odds board as Spider's horse dropped from forty-to-one to twenty-two on the last flash.

By the time the field was halfway down the backstretch, the horse was at least a dozen lengths in front and as he passed Ham and Willie at the sixteenth pole, Spider snuck a peek back between his legs, saw that he was safely home and turned down his whip.

"He posed nice for the photo finish camera," said Willie and when the track photographer took the winner's circle picture only the groom and the hotwalker were there, with the trainer and his entourage nowhere to be seen.

Monday morning a vet came by and took x-rays of Mighty's knees and ankles and pulled off his shoes so they could do his feet too and Willie shook his head and said it's just like Bogie said would happen, Mister Russo's kids are selling my big horse for a pile of money.

The next day Bogie told Willie to do the colt up in shipping bandages because he'd be sending him on the night flight out to the west coast and not to worry, they were all going to get a piece of the commission but by the day Willie and Ham were set to ship to Keeneland with J.B.'s horses neither one had seen a dime.

Willie said not to be surprised whenever that happens since lots of folks make promises about money, but when it gets in their pocket and it's their money they forget about you and that's the reason you can't take promises to the bank.

CHAPTER 8

Those eighteen wheel vans they used for long trips could hold a dozen horses but most trainers would only send eight or sometimes less and often they would ask for a stall and a half or a box stall so the animals could stretch out. And the drivers always tried to take the most direct route to wherever they were headed, since the horses had no choice but to stand for the whole ride and most didn't mind it but when they were racing fit some would get a bit antsy.

Coming out of Florida in early April from Hialeah they travelled from the heat and humidity, up through Georgia past Atlanta and on by Knoxville, Tennessee, a trip of over a thousand miles to the cooler air in Lexington, Kentucky that can take almost twenty hours, so they needed someone to ride with the horses, check their water buckets and make sure they have some hay to nibble at, even if it was only to give them something to relieve the boredom.

Willie knew a couple of the grooms that worked for J.B. and they all seemed okay with him being the new assistant trainer, maybe more so since he rode the van along with them and they all liked that his way was to suggest things rather than bark orders like a lot of bosses do.

He told Ham to ride on one of the other trucks so he'd get to know the guys and some of the horses they'd be working with.

There were eight horses on Ham's van and darned if Suzy's Song wasn't one of them, standing among the other fillies and mares with a tag on her halter that said "Spendthrift Farm."

"I used to rub this filly," said Ham to the guy who was looking after her.

"She's all done racing, going off to get bred," said the guy.

When the vans stopped and they got off to stretch their legs Ham told Willie about Suzie being on the van and Willie said likely she was going to a fine stallion since she was a stakes winner and he bet it was Raise A Native, the best one there.

When they got back on the road again that was something Ham talked to Suzy about as he hand-fed her some alfalfa. She never did carry much weight and Ham made sure he checked on her every once in a while, rubbing her withers and telling her what a good race mare she'd been and how pretty soon she'd have a nice baby to run alongside her in those fields of long sweet bluegrass.

The trip felt endless and tiresome since it was nearly non-stop, not like the ride from Belmont to Hialeah when they could break up the overnight with a respite in South Carolina.

This time the vans left mid-morning but after they made a pass through Ocala to swap out a couple of horses that were due for a rest for a couple that were ready to run, they rolled along at a pretty good pace through those same swamps and lowlands Ham had been fascinated by on his way south.

When they crossed the Tennessee River and passed through Knoxville it began to remind him of home back in New England, the dark green leaves of the hardwoods and tall pines on the sides of the Smokey Mountains, some of which were even taller than the ones Ham had known back in Vermont.

He used his pocketknife to cut a piece of string off a hay bale and he tied it around his wrist to remind him to write to his mom when he got to Kentucky.

The sun was already up for an hour or so when they rolled through Richmond, Kentucky and Ham saw a road sign for Lexington, and shortly after he spotted another that said Keeneland. They took a left onto the New Circle Road and when the caravan exited for the Versailles Road, Ham was lucky to be looking out the window on the right side of the van.

Between two white stone pillars each topped by an iron eagle with its wings spread wide, an elaborate gate painted bright red was guarding the entrance to Calumet Farm.

Miles and miles of white four-board fence trailed across the rolling hills of sprawling paddocks and Ham counted thirty mares and foals before the van passed by Calumet and climbed another hill.

There was a little airport to the left and out his window he could see the stone walls that flanked the entry to Keeneland race track as they passed. The driver braked softly and made a wide right turn onto Van Meter Road and pulled through the back stable gate to the loading ramps.

"First track I ever stepped my foot on," said Willie,

"Daddy brought me here when I was two and he was working for Mister John E. Madden, out at Hamburg Place Stud over in Winchester. They called that man the 'Wizard of the Turf' and that's what he was. He forgot more about a horse than most folks will ever get to know."

"It's kind of out in the sticks here," said Ham.

Willie told him yessir and it would be a hike and a half to get anywhere to go eat, but the food in the track kitchen was Southern cooking almost as good as what he made himself.

"You're going to put on a few pounds, Mister Ham," he said, "when you get to eating them biscuits with that red-eye gravy for breakfast."

They gave each of the horses a short walk and a little graze before they put them away, but when they did, most wanted to lie right down and doze, and some did just that for the rest of the day.

And when a van driver came to shuttle Suzy off to Spendthrift Farm he told Ham there were lots of mares going there to get bred and he'd take him over to see the place next time he came back to pick up another one.

The tack rooms weren't as big as the ones at Belmont or Hialeah, but neither Willie nor Ham were toting along much in the way of possessions. Ham's collection of a dozen books fit neatly on one shelf in an old black steamer trunk he had found at the Bird Road flea market by Tropical Park and he could still get the rest of his clothes in the duffel bag he'd left home with.

When they felt like they had the shedrow looking ship-shape, Willie and Ham took a walk up the hill to see the race track and Ham said how come the stands face west like that, wouldn't you have the sun in your eyes in the afternoon, and Willie said that's the way the land lay so that's the way they built it.

But it had the feel of Saratoga, old and classy, and when they climbed the steps to the grandstand they sat there for a while in the open seats and watched the setting sun and it reminded Ham of how they did that the first week he came around.

Before it got dark they walked through a paddock that was similar to the one at Saratoga and had numbers on the trees, except it was much smaller and had a white fence surrounding it to keep the spectators out of the way.

The other barns were filled and Willie knew lots of folks there, stopping to chat and introduce Ham and he did it with some degree of formality, and when they moved on all of them said goodbye to "Mister Ham and Eggs."

When they got back to the barn, Ham cut the string off his wrist and told Willie he needed to write a letter home and Willie said since it's to your momma, you go on ahead and do that and I'll bring you back some supper from the kitchen.

Ham had a lot of catching up to do, not being in touch for the whole winter except the few lines on a Christmas card he'd sent with a hundred dollar bill for his mom to buy presents for herself and the girls and the short phone call he made on Christmas Eve when he got just a touch homesick.

He told her that he was doing fine, that he worked for another outfit now and planned to come back to Saratoga in

August and he promised he'd take some time to come home and see everyone.

It wasn't as long a letter as the one he sent from Belmont but he told her all about how Avalanche had won at Tropical Park and Suzy's dead heat in the stakes race and how that was something even Willie had never done.

And he didn't mention Carla, probably because it bothered him to think about her too much, especially since he hadn't heard a peep from her since she went off to California, and he for sure didn't say anything about Lizzie telling him she wanted to get married because that was way too confusing for him at the moment.

It seemed they had something to run every day that first week at Keeneland since J.B. wasn't one to leave his horses sitting in the barn, because like he said they don't make any money eating hay.

The first two were off the board, but on the opening Saturday Ham walked a chestnut colt named Daddy's Donegone up the hill and stood next to J.B. and Willie as they watched him come from last to first and break the ice for them.

And you could hardly get near the TV in the grandstand to watch as Secretariat looped those horses and took the Gotham Stakes easily, leaving the gate at odds of one-to-nine and Willie said he'd have an easy job in the Wood Memorial before he came to Kentucky.

To celebrate their first win, J.B. had one of his buddies bring a big spread to the barn and Ham filled himself up with barbecued ribs and chicken and corn on the cob and he even drank a beer from the keg and nobody seemed to care and when he laid his head on the pillow that night he asked Willie if Kentucky might be another name for heaven.

Willie was right about the food, and maybe it was growing pains, but Ham found himself jogging off to the kitchen a couple of times each day for a snack and if he hadn't started making his late afternoon run around the track he probably would have put on those pounds Willie talked about.

J.B. was a big guy who wore a cowboy hat and boots and jeans and a starched white shirt all the time and he commented that Ham better get a pair of those boots so he could be looking his boss in the eye and too bad he wasn't a football player or those Kentucky Wildcats would be dragging him off to play for the university over there in Lexington.

He drove a Cadillac unlike any Ham had ever seen, this one with the back chopped off like a pickup truck where he liked to throw bales of hay and straw or anything else that needed toting. It was a big, fancy version of the

Chevy El Caminos or the Ford Rancheros that a lot of other racetrackers drove, but it was for sure a one-of-a-kind, especially since it was painted purple to match J.B.'s racing colors, with a yellow flame on the doors meant to evoke his last name, Burns.

And J.B. did like to make a sizeable bet once in a while, not the way most folks did, a hundred or a couple of hundred. He'd bet that way at the windows and Willie said the man might put up ten or twenty thousand with the bookies but you couldn't tell by watching him since he'd never blink, win or lose. Willie remembered when he'd been standing next to J.B. when he lost a big one and the most sign he gave of being upset was to say "Shoot, that wasn't so good" and "let's go get us a hot dog and a beer."

Willie said he knew for a fact J.B. had bet twenty thousand one Kentucky Derby day on one of his maidens. J.B. said that was the best day all year to lay it in heavy since everybody in America liked to gamble on horses on Derby day whether they knew a horse from a billy-goat and the betting pools were as fat as possible with what he called dead money.

Like a lot of trainers that raced in Kentucky, J.B. looked and acted like a cowboy, and folks thought he was from way out west, Montana or Wyoming or even Texas but the license plate on his car said Kansas. He was proud to be a Jayhawk and had a farm outside of Kansas City where he'd go to rest up every once in a while and he bred some Quarter horses there to run at Eureka Downs.

It was lunchtime on a Saturday, the day of the Bluegrass stakes and folks were starting to get what Willie said was "Derby fever," some thinking that Secretariat being beat four lengths in the Wood Memorial the week before might mean the door was open for anybody with a good horse.

Forego would be a slight favorite over Royal and Regal in the Bluegrass and Willie said he was going to make a little bet on him, not risking much because of the odds, but if he won he'd parlay it back and turn a little into a lot the next time the big gelding ran.

Ham said he'd probably watch or maybe bet five bucks on that jock Angel Cordero, Jr. that he liked so much at Belmont.

They had just returned from lunch when J.B. waved Willie and Ham into his office at the end of the barn.

"Make a little bet for me, would you fellas?" he said.

"Yessir," said Willie.

"Yessir," said Ham.

On J.B.'s desk was a pile of cash.

"Twenty-five hundred to win and twenty-five hundred to place," he said, "on that colt My Gallant that Angel rides."

And he told them to put the money in a few hundred at a time, since the horse was a longshot and we were talking about a lot of cash here.

Walking around with all those Ben Franklins in his pocket made Ham a little nervous but he stayed close to Willie and put the bets in with a couple of trips to the fifty-dollar window while Willie went to the hundred. And they each made a bet for themselves, since Willie said you never go wrong following a lucky wagon and J.B. sure was one of those.

They hung at the fence as the horses loaded in the gate and nobody who saw Forego could take their eyes off him, but when the horses broke from the gate and headed into the first turn Blum sent Royal and Regal right to the lead and opened up a couple of lengths on the field.

"Mousey's gonna try and steal it," said Willie and since Keeneland didn't have an announcer, if you didn't pay attention the race might go off and the only way you'd know the horses were running was by hearing the crowd cheer.

Ham listened to Willie but his eyes weren't on the leader but on the horse with the white and red silks glued to the rail a few lengths behind, as Cordero rated My Gallant in hopes of getting the jump on them at the top of the stretch and that was exactly what he did, opening up some ground there and hanging on to win by a neck.

"Ole Forego never got hisself untracked," said Willie, and it was the first time Ham had seen the old man sweating like that.

It took them until the last race was over to cash all the tickets, Ham's five hundred turning into over six thousand and making his head swim. As they walked back to the barn he felt as if he were a foot taller than Willie and whatever they were talking about he sure couldn't recall by the time they got there.

Shorty made good on his promise to Ham when J.B. decided one of the maiden fillies couldn't cut it as a racehorse because she was too slow and told the owner maybe she'd make a good broodmare for having such a fine pedigree.

Ham rode up front in the van and Shorty turned the trip across town into a guided tour after they left Spendthrift as they continued on to drop off mares and pick other ones up at Calumet and Bluegrass Farm and Gainesway and Claiborne before they headed back to the track.

Ham was struck by the vastness of the farms, the endless rolling paddocks fencing in mares that grazed in deep green grass halfway up to their knees and Shorty told him they had it pretty good but not as good as the stud horses who got pampered like kings and how it would be great to be one of them.

And how the one you wouldn't want to be was what they called the "Teaser," which was the male horse that got the mares warmed up and in the mood and got taken away before he got to do anything before the stallion came in for the lovemaking. <u>That</u> was a rotten job, he said.

At supper that night Ham asked Willie why some horses got to be breeding stock and others didn't and Willie said it's all about blood and money, why they say they breed the best to the best and hope for the best, which would mean either winning a big race or selling them for tons of cash at the auctions.

J.B. lived life like it was a stage show, driving his fancy purple Cadillac and wearing those ostrich cowboy boots and a purple satin jacket around the track in order that everyone would recognize him and he said it was important to toot your own horn when you did something good like win a race, 'cause it wasn't sure anyone would pay attention if you didn't.

But when it came to making money, J.B. liked to do the opposite of what folks would think. He'd never go wager himself and if he did, it was likely he was trying to throw off those guys who'd follow him to the betting windows and he said they'd all do that once, lose their money and never bother him again. Sometimes when he'd be leaving the paddock one of the railbirds would come right out and ask him if he was going to win and he'd wink at them and say "bet your mortgage, bud," but only when the horse was going to run poorly.

Willie said J.B.'s father taught him that, back when they raced at small tracks where the purses were so small that they had to cash a ticket once in a while just to stay in business and every point in the odds counted for a lot of real money. And when he went to the horse sales to buy young horses to resell, Willie said you could never tell which one he was interested in, 'cause he'd just touch the brim of his hat when he bid.

Once or twice a week J.B. would bring folks to the barn and he'd tell Willie to pull out one of the horses he was trying to sell, talking all the while about the thrill of winning a big race to the men in expensive suits and their wives that would be wearing furs and diamonds.

J.B. would pull a bottle of champagne from the refrigerator in his office and they'd toast to hope for some luck to bless the deal before those fancy people would step up and buy one, and that was all what he called selling the sizzle first and the steak afterwards.

But J.B. was all heart when it came to his own people. He made sure the barn help got taken care of with a few dollars when he won a race and if they got sick he sent them to a doctor and he even helped a lot of them put their kids through school.

He asked Ham if he had been to college and when Ham said no, J.B. said that's a shame, a smart kid like you should have an education, maybe you'd run this whole show some day.

Keeneland's spring meet only lasted three weeks and as soon as they closed the doors the ones at Churchill Downs were ready to open and for J.B.'s stable that meant it was time to pack up and head back east.

J.B. said he'd like to stick around for the Derby if he had one in it or something to bet on that day, but this year that wasn't happening.

The stable had half-a-dozen wins during the time they spent in Kentucky and everybody's pockets were full so J.B. gave a couple of the grooms time off to go home to Mexico and see their families before they had to show up at Belmont and he told Willie to go on ahead and train the horses easy until he got there, he was heading to the farm in Kansas for a couple of weeks to freshen up.

They loaded the equipment and before they put the horses on the vans everyone sat down for a barbecue outside the barn while they gathered around a TV and watched Secretariat romp home a winner in the Kentucky Derby and Willie didn't say I told you so but he did point out how Big Red had run every quarter mile faster than the previous one, and said that was something no horse had ever done before.

Ham stood and tapped on his glass like he was the master of ceremonies at a banquet, ready to make a speech:

"The week I came around the track last year Willie told me that red horse'd win the Triple Crown and I bet he does."

And nobody would take that bet since they all agreed, even those guys who always argued about everything, the ones Willie said would knock motherhood and apple pie.

But they didn't knock Secretariat.

CHAPTER 9

The vans left Kentucky before dark and followed a direct route east through the Blue Ridge Mountains of West Virginia and northern Maryland as they skirted the length of Pennsylvania.

"Fifty thousand men lost their lives yonder," said Willie when they passed the turnoff for Gettysburg and when they passed Antietam he said another twenty three thousand had died there and next time they were at Saratoga he'd show Ham the battlefield where the Americans won their first battle in the war for independence.

The trip to Belmont went so smoothly that it was barely mid-morning when Willie had all the horses put up in their stalls and gathered the help to enjoy a big breakfast spread that J.B. paid for as a custom when they shipped to a new track.

"That's why everybody wants to work for this outfit," said Willie, "The man is first class."

And Willie did what his boss told him, trained the horses easy and the few they did run were entered in tough spots that they didn't figure to win and he told the riders not to beat them up for nothing, but if they could win, he said go on ahead and try but none did.

Spider had an agent that Willie liked who kept coming around asking for mounts so Willie put him on a three year old colt named Homestead that he said would need a couple of more sprints before they sent him around two turns which was what his pedigree said he wanted.

The horse dragged Spider to the lead and opened up a couple of lengths before fading and Willie said that was just what the doctor ordered but he didn't put the kid on any more horses.

"He's got the devil's mark," said Willie after he saw the dark spot in Spider's palm when he reached to shake hands in the paddock. He told Ham that confirmed what he'd been thinking about Spider, that he had an evil streak and no good would ever come of him.

Ham was rubbing a pair of maiden two year olds, a chestnut filly called Blitzie and a bay colt named Truly Hot and each of them looked like they might be a runner. And he had an old grey gelding named Bolder Dan who only ran on the turf and was the one that J.B. said was his favorite horse in the barn because he'd cashed so many bets on him.

Ham figured they would all be ready to run when the boss got back and in the meantime he busied himself helping Willie shape up the barn, which meant new flowers in the flower beds and fresh sod and sand for the walking ring. And they shined up the purple wall plaques outside the barn and the ones by each of the horses' stalls.

When J.B. showed up, the back of his Caddy was filled with coolers, all stuffed with butchered ribs cut from the prime cattle he ran on his spread in Kansas, and right away he had a party at the barn for not just his help but their families too and Ham watched as he spent time to visit with all of them and knew everyone's name.

J.B. seemed energized from that respite in Kansas and he went to running horses in every spot he could find, sometimes shipping one down to Monmouth or up to Rockingham where the great Jack Van Berg was the leading trainer.

They had a purple six-horse van and it seemed like they were loading a runner on it every day. For the next month and a half Ham got to be a travelling man, driving the van and taking whatever horse was running to the paddock where either J.B. or Willie would show up and put the saddle on.

For a short spell the barn's luck went bone dry and nothing would win, no matter how many new pennies Willie threw in the infield lake or how many little kids Ham rubbed on their heads. It seemed that every time one of the horses made the lead, they ran out of gas in the stretch and got caught or if they were charging from the back of the pack, they'd get to the finish line one jump too late.

Ham drove the van up to Rockingham on a Sunday and when Bolder Dan got headed at the sixteenth pole Ham thought sure he was beat but the old boy charged back and stuck his nose in front just as they hit the wire like he knew right where it was, and that turned the streak around.

J.B. and Willie were both busy, so Ham asked Mister Van Berg to saddle for him and when they took the winner's circle photo Ham was alone in the picture with the horse and rider and it looked like he was the trainer instead of a groom, there with that big smile plastered on his face.

For the next two weeks it seemed as if all they had to do was take a horse to the paddock and put the saddle on and it would win and J.B. went to betting big on everything they ran even if he thought they couldn't win, 'cause what did he know anyway and when the racing gods are in your corner, nothing can stop you.

One morning Ham spotted a blonde girl at the end of the shedrow and thought for a second it was Lizzie and he called out hey to her but it turned out it was another girl, one who worked for the tack company, trying to get some business from J.B.

They had been there for almost a month and Lizzie still hadn't showed and Willie said maybe she married a rich guy and went to live in a big fancy house and Ham laughed but he didn't really know how he felt about that.

Ham chatted up the tack girl a few times when she was dropping off new brushes or some of those white bridles J.B. used so he could always see where his horses were in the race, and she told him her name was Molly and when Ham asked her if she'd like to catch a movie sometime she said maybe.

After one of the two year olds jumped a dark spot on the track in the middle of a workout, J.B. sent Ham to the tack shop to get a shadow roll and Molly was there and he heard her call the old man behind the desk Daddy, and that made it clear how things stood right away.

Ham made sure to say have a good morning sir to her Daddy before he left and he thought maybe that was a good thing by the wink he got from Molly and the next weekend she went with him to see the new James Bond movie.

She said it was almost her favorite because it was set in New Orleans and she and her father went there to the Fair Grounds track every winter but the James Bond she really liked was that Scottish guy that played 007 before.

Blitzie and Truly Hot were only two year olds, and two year olds don't usually run a lot before July but these were ready to run early because of the way J.B. liked to get his babies out before the competition got too tough. Willie said every once in a while he would even have them ready at Keeneland in April, so watch out, in the middle of summer any of them might win at any time.

J.B. told Ham he was going to enter Blitzie the next Saturday coming which was Belmont Day and that figured to be the biggest crowd-draw in racing, the race coming up with only four horses trying to stand between Secretariat and Triple Crown history.

Secretariat had whipped everyone so badly in the Derby and the Preakness that Willie said he'd be one to nine and that was the only day in history you could make a case for betting on a one to nine shot since Big Red could fall down and still get back up to beat any of those horses.

In any case, he said you should go buy a two dollar win ticket and not cash it, just to remind you of the day you saw a Triple Crown winner, 'cause there won't be many of those that you do see in your lifetime.

Ham suspected J.B. might be getting ready to make a bet on Blitzie after he'd told him to take the filly over to the paddock and school her between races. That was because he didn't want her to get shook up on Belmont day when the crowd would be five deep around the walking ring and some fans who didn't know any better would hoot and holler at the horses like they were at a rodeo.

But what made Ham sure they were going for the money was right before they left the barn and Willie showed him a set of blinkers and said oh boy we'll be having some fun today. So Ham went to the tack room and climbed up to the rafters and he dug into his stash and pulled out two hundred for a win bet and another two hundred for the place and stuck it in his left front shirt pocket.

Sixty-something thousand people packed themselves into Belmont that June afternoon, folks giddy at the chance they'd be seeing the first Triple winner in a long generation and they were everywhere, camped on the landings and sitting on the stairs and some with blankets spread on the ground like they were having a picnic or a day at the beach.

The banner planes were back and the mood was ecstatic, almost as if Secretariat had already won, so enraptured were his fans.

Blitzie was on her toes, bouncing when they left the barn, but halfway over to the paddock Willie told Ham to hold up while he put her blinkers on and she settled down nicely with her game face on.

They passed the horses coming back from the first race and Ham asked one of the grooms who'd won it and he said that bug boy Spider did and when Ham looked in his program he saw the horse had been a big longshot on the morning line so he asked what had it paid.

"Sixty-four dollars," the guy yelled back over his shoulder as his horse dragged him down the ramp that went through the tunnel to the stable area.

There's always a buzz on the big race days, those days when the track is packed and there's a festival-like feeling to the place and in some way running in any race on that day has a bit of the same electricity of the big race and that was what Ham was feeling with Blitzie even though she was just a maiden.

J.B. pulled a long piece of gauze from his pocket and as he started to wrap the tongue-tie on the filly, Willie said boss she never wore one before, and J.B. said don't you worry, she's wearing one today, just go bet your money.

When J.B. tightened the girth, Ham felt her take another breath and he stretched her front legs and rubbed her cheek to make sure she'd know he was right there, still connected to her with the shank. He gave her a turn around the walking ring before the other horses got out and she stepped lively, not with any nervousness, just intent on getting on.

Cordero took advantage of being in the inside post as they left the gate at the five furlong pole and he sent Blitzie right out and hugged the rail to open up a couple of lengths. When a big grey that was at least a head taller came to her at the top of the stretch, Cordero eased her off the wood to float his pursuer wide and then wider, but they never made contact as they straightened in the lane and he hung on to win by a long neck.

And J.B. was arrayed in purple from head to toe, except for the white cowboy hat that he took off and waved at the crowd from the winner's circle. Ham looked around at the others and realized that he was looking down on J. B. and the rest and his filly too, that recurring feeling of towering over the crowd but when the photographer said smile he forgot all about it.

The following week when Ham saw the winner's circle photo, it occurred to him that he'd had that "big" feeling then but you couldn't tell anything looking at the picture.

Blitzie was still bouncing at the test barn and she took forever to pee but they never rushed the horses after a race, always giving them a bath and some time to graze before they put them away. So it was lucky for Ham and Willie that their only runner was in an early race and that allowed them enough time to get back over to the frontside in time to watch Secretariat perform.

And it was a good thing that Ham and Willie were tall guys, otherwise they wouldn't have been able to see over the crowd at the paddock and be part of the gentle roar that went up when the big chestnut passed by, the one who had become the people's hero.

They got a spot right on the outside fence to watch the race, there by the starting gate and they both sang along with the crowd:

"*East side, West side... all around the town...*" and there was another gentle roar when the five horses broke from the gate.

But Willie said afterward that in all his years on the track, nothing he had ever seen before had prepared him for the race he saw that day, Secretariat loping along on the lead, putting away Sham half way through the race and widening his lead with every other stride he took from there to the finish.

"Race horses come and go, but the great ones stay in your heart forever," said Willie and as Secretariat crossed the wire, Ham once again felt himself floating above the crowd, looking down on the chaos.

Ham preferred to go for his jogs late in the day when the sun was low and he could immerse himself in the vastness of the long, broad Belmont track.

It was almost half again as long as Hialeah and Keeneland and probably twice as wide so he'd do two laps before supper most evenings and three every once in a while. By the time he finished, he was all sweated up and he started wearing a towel around his neck like the jockeys who were doing the same thing to keep their weight down.

Once in a while he'd run with them, but those guys were serious athletes and even if his legs were a lot longer than theirs he still had to push himself hard just to stay close.

He'd finished three times around and was by the winners circle running water from a hose over his head when one of the jockeys that was wearing a rubber suit to pull some weight asked him would he like to come to a party and said you can count on plenty of food there, 'cause the rest of us are on a diet.

The house where the jockey lived wasn't that far away, over in Floral Park where a lot of racetrack people lived so Ham walked there and as he strolled in who was there among the others but Spider, sporting a white silk shirt and dark linen slacks and alligator shoes. Spider was at the bar by the swimming pool drinking whiskey from a crystal glass, pouring the Crown Royal for himself and he had a pretty girl hanging all over him, one that might have been even prettier without the dyed black hair and darkened eyes.

"Down to one bug, five pounds," said Spider, meaning that his weight allowance had been cut to half of what he'd started with now that he'd won his thirty-fifth race. Spider was feeling high on himself and the rest of their conversation was mostly a critique of his fellow jockeys, how some didn't get low enough, some didn't finish strong like he did.

"You shoulda' called me when I told you to," said Spider, "we made a ton on those ones my old man shipped from down south."

Ham wasn't sure if it was just the whiskey talking when Spider told him another Argentine horse he'd ride next weekend would ring the bell, just before he drew another drink and lurched off, summoned by a couple of guys who looked a lot like the ones Ham had seen him with in Florida the day he won that first race.

The patio deck held an eclectic group of everything from older men in silk suits to young women in short skirts and heels mixed in with the jockeys and wet bikini-girls fresh from the pool. Rock music pounded from the stereo speakers and there was a smell of reefer mixed in with the cigarette smoke, and some of the girls laughed that nervous cocaine-laugh.

Ham felt about as comfortable as a boy scout in a biker bar around those guys in the suits when their women looked him up and down and smiled.

"You got a girlfriend, honey?" asked one.

"I did, but she went to California," said Ham and when she asked him if he was looking for another one, he said not now thanks and moved away.

A couple of times he got that strange feeling of being a foot or two taller than everyone and the sounds were modulating but he hadn't had any drugs and just sipped at a beer, so he figured it was just one of those things that came and went and he never thought about it again.

After an hour or so of small talk with the few folks he'd recognized from the track he put the rest of that beer he'd been nursing on the bar, said his good-byes to the jock that invited him and slipped out the door.

Willie was sleeping hard when Ham got back to Belmont that night, so it wasn't until breakfast in the track kitchen next morning that he told him about the party.

They talked about that high-flying lifestyle that those drinking, smoking, drug-taking people were living.

"A lot of those people believe in heaven and they figure you can have it in this life or the next but they're not the kind that have much faith so they take it in this one in case there isn't any next," said Willie.

"Spider kind of fit right in," said Ham.

And he told Willie that Spider had bragged about those big payoffs on horses that looked on paper like they had no chance at all and said he had another one coming up soon that he planned to make a big score on.

"Your boy Spider might have layed himself down with some dirty dogs," said Willie and he reminded Ham what he said before about fish keeping their mouths shut and how that might apply to Spider, especially with the kind of gentlemen he was choosing to spend his time with.

Something Ham always had on his mind was what Willie told him about the race track life, how it was just like the circus and no matter how you did at one meet, pretty soon you got to pick up your tent and go to the next and if it wasn't so great now just wait.

He wondered if that was how racetrackers reconciled the fact that most horses lose more races than they win, but that didn't make you a loser. Quite the contrary, he thought, considering that on the face of things a trainer who won twenty percent of their starts was considered a huge success, even though that meant he was losing eighty percent of the time.

Their outfit was rolling along fine at Belmont, winning at a good clip and horses were paying good prices when they did bet and some of the ones that were losing went off at too short a price to bet anyway which saved everyone some money.

J.B. said Fourth of July weather was going to be as hot as a firecracker and that's when the track folks started talking about Saratoga, how it was so much cooler up there in the mountains and how August couldn't come soon enough.

Ham knew that it could be just as hot and humid up north, but pretty soon he bought into the notion too and found himself just as anxious as everyone else, besides he wanted to get back closer to home.

Before they left Belmont J.B. did something almost no one else would, running Truly Hot first time out in a stakes race, and the little bay showed himself well, making the lead and only getting beat a couple of lengths and J.B. said that was a good way to get our feet wet, now we'll go hunting big game up at the Spa.

After Secretariat won easily in Chicago Ham read Joe Hirsch's story in the *Morning Telegraph* to Willie, the great scribe saying how Big Red's folks were planning to bring him back to Saratoga and that would be like the homecoming of a native son since the Spa was where he broke his maiden and they might shatter all the records for attendance that day and maybe have thirty thousand people there and Willie just smiled at that and said:

"You and me, Ham and Eggs, we'll be up on the second floor."

J.B. stabled his horses in the main barn area at Saratoga, not across Union Avenue at Oklahoma where Mister Evans kept his, and as the vans rolled up US 9, Ham happened to be looking out the left side of the trailer as it passed the bus stop in front of the Spa City Diner where he'd disembarked on his journey from Vermont.

The vans turned off before they got to Canfield's Casino and the park where Hamilton Greer spent his first night in Saratoga on a wooden bench, but seeing that diner and the bus stop and the path he'd taken made it feel like a hundred years had passed instead of just one and he nearly couldn't imagine it had been him, the kid that walked down that hill and stood on the corner of Caroline Street and Broadway.

They were there for about a week when Willie asked Ham if maybe he would like to take a couple of days off to go home to see his mama. Ham had been thinking about just that ever since they arrived in Saratoga, but he kept putting it off, not sure how he'd feel when he saw everyone, that maybe he'd now become a different person and that it might be strange and uncomfortable.

Both of Ham's two year olds were going to run in stakes races, so he tried to use that to justify his reluctance to leave, saying J.B. was counting on him.

"Get on up there and see your family," said Willie, pointing out that a two hour bus ride wasn't a trip to the moon and besides, those horses would still be there when he got back

Ham phoned to tell his mom he'd be coming on the following Sunday but he made her promise not to say what time he'd arrive because he wanted to make it a surprise for Abby and Ella and Jennie and Anna and he'd take the noon bus so as to be there when the girls came home from working brunch at the Inn.

His mom said Abe Lincoln's great-granddaughter still lived at Hildene, the family estate about a mile from where Hamilton grew up and the Orvis shop was right where it always was and so was the Manchester Inn but he grimaced when the bus passed the old Equinox hotel and it was shuttered and closed up tight.

And he was excited to give his sisters the gifts he brought from Florida, trinkets like orange snow-globes and fake alligators since none of them knew anything more about the south than what they read in the encyclopedia.

But they were already home when he got there, his sisters and step-sisters waiting on the front porch when he walked up the driveway, screaming like he was either a war hero or the prodigal son and his mom and Steve ran right out too when they heard the ruckus.

Ham wasn't sure how it would go, coming home to the place he'd left in such a hurry, after some words exchanged that both sides might now regret.

But his mother couldn't stop talking, so much was she crying and laughing at the same time to see her boy, grown up and filled out so, and Steve did the respectful thing, treating him like a man and shaking his hand and telling Ham they'd all missed him.

Hamilton's mom made his favorite dinner, roast leg of lamb and mint jelly with potatoes and string beans and they lingered at the table for a while as they finished off the apple pie stepsister Jenny had made.

After dinner Steve made a point of getting everyone to walk together down the hill to town center to work off the heavy meal but mainly to give them all a chance to chat.

Most of the time Ham felt he was the only one talking, going on about Willie and J.B. and the horses he'd taken care of in the past year, and he told them about Spider and mentioned Lizzie and Molly which drew question after question from the girls but he didn't say anything about Carla.

By the time they got back to the house the lightning bugs were glowing on the front lawn and Steve brought out a few extra rocking chairs and soon everyone had parked themselves there on the front porch, right where they were when Ham arrived. When they were alone in the kitchen for a few minutes he gave his mom an envelope with five hundred dollars in it and told her to put it towards the girls' college fund and she looked in the envelope and began to cry.

It was near midnight when he told them he had to catch the noon bus back to Saratoga because a couple of the horses he took care of were going to run in important races but if they wanted to make an outing, he'd get some passes for them and maybe they'd come on down and watch his horses run.

Secretariat was a one-to-nine favorite on the odds board when he went in the gate for the Whitney Handicap, and carrying only 119 pounds, and Willie said it should be a walk in the park, but Jacinto Vasquez sent a little horse named Onion to the lead and that crowd of folks there to root for the champ was so shocked you could have heard a cricket chirp after Onion hung on to beat Big Red.

Willie just shook his head...

"Shoulda' known it would be him that would beat him, he already done whipped Kelso and Buckpasser. He kills all the giants, that Mister Jerkens."

Three more times that fall Ham and Willie got to see Secretariat run at Belmont, once when he won the Marlboro Cup by three and a half lengths and another when he finished five in front after a mile and a half on the grass in the Man o' War.

But between those two victories he went to the post odds-on in the Woodward on a rainy, sloppy day.

"Got me a bad feeling today, son," said Willie, "Big Red better watch out Mister Jerkens don't upset his apple cart again."

And Mister Jerkens told his jockey not to be shy, just go on and take it right to him and send that Prove Out, maybe you'll get the mile and a half better than he does today.

And that's exactly what he did.

PART II

CHAPTER 10

1974-75

Ham was glad to be in Kentucky in April, when the
Dogwood trees unfolded their pink and white blossoms and
folks put aside memories of what a cold, dreary winter it
had been, grateful to be rewarded with such a glorious
morning at the Keeneland track.

Ham and Willie were in a box seat at the finish line
clocking the two-year old colt that J.B. said was the best in
his crop that year:

"You boys go ahead and stick Calvin Borel on to blow
him out three-eighths and we'll get the money as soon as I
get back from the farm."

Borel jogged the big bay the wrong way past the
seven-eighths pole and turned him and let him stand for a
few moments before they galloped on, and by the time they
dropped to the rail at the three furlong pole, they were
rolling.

As he crossed the finish line the rider eased up a bit and Willie showed Ham his stopwatch.

"Thirty-five flat..." he said, laughing,

"You can't make a good horse work slow."

"He won't be much of a secret now," said Ham, meaning that the clockers must have seen the same thing they did and likely the cat was out of the bag.

"C'mon, walk this way," said Willie and they headed toward the other end of the stands as the rider walked their colt towards the tunnel that led from the winners circle to the paddock, which was hardly the direct way home, but a path that took them past a lone figure with a couple of watches and a clipboard.

"Mornin', Cole," said Willie to the white-haired clocker.

"Looked like thirty-seven and one on Buster Brown," said the man with a wink, and Willie gave him back a nod.

Buster Brown broke on the lead and opened up four and stayed there to the wire and it was a good thing Keeneland had such a big winners circle considering the crowd of friends J.B. had in tow. Ham led the colt in and stood him with his head high and his legs straight and J.B. set everyone in place for the picture and wiped the colt's face with a sponge as he took the tongue-tie off. The fans crowded the fence and whistled and for a moment or two

Ham had the sensation again that he was bigger, taller than the rest and looking down on them below.

And even if it was only a maiden race, the soul of Keeneland was tradition and one of their most cherished traditions had always been to present a silver julep cup to winning owners and J.B. held his cup high as if it were the actual Kentucky Derby trophy because when you win one of those maidens with a two year old, that's what's immediately in the back of everybody's mind, next year's Derby.

They caught a ride over to a little joint called Buffalo and Dads with one of the guys on the gate crew named Speck who swore it was the best place in town if you wanted to get some liver and onions for supper and Ham waited until Speck went to the men's room before he told Willie what was on his mind.

"I was thinking maybe I'd like to buy myself a horse," he said and Willie laughed.

"And I was wondering when you'd want to do just that," said Willie, "Either that or a car."

"I've got the money," said Ham.

"Better a horse than a car... cars can't win you no money," said Willie and Ham said he'd get around to a car later but right now he didn't have anywhere to go.

Ham said he had been keeping an eye on a horse that he knew from back in New York, one of the Bucky Lane mares that never had enough to eat and the guy who was training him now wanted out and told him that twenty-five hundred would buy her. Ham said Spider rode the horse a few times and word on the backstretch was that he was in bed with some race fixers and the poor horse probably didn't know if she was supposed to go or supposed to whoa.

"She sound?" said Willie and Ham nodded yes.

"Then tell him you'll give two thousand, cash," said Willie and Ham did that next morning and brought the ribby grey mare home along with a bill of sale and her foal papers signed over to him.

They worked a deal with J.B. that Ham could rub her along with his other three and when she was ready to run, J.B. would saddle for him and run her in his colors, but Ham had to get his owner's license and pay for feed and he could cover all the vet and blacksmith and horse dentist bills out of his paycheck.

For a mare with such a fancy name Proper Princess wasn't much to look at. Her coat was as dull as the back of the barn and her ribs looked like they were painted on.

The first day Ham had her she dug a hole two feet deep in her stall and chewed the top board off the door. He thought for sure he'd bought himself a cribber, but Willie told him she was just lonely and bored and underfed and not sucking air.

"You go get her a rubber ball and hang it from the ceiling and rub a little cayenne pepper on the stall door and watch if she doesn't stop that gnawing," said Willie,

"We'll put her on some sweet-feed and throw some alfalfa in the corner every once in a while, and maybe you'll have you a Cinderella."

Ham took Princess out late in the morning, after all the other work was done and an exercise girl from Kentucky named Hayley said she thought it was nice he wasn't a jerk like a lot of guys on the backstretch and she'd be happy to gallop that mare if Ham wanted to buy her dinner once in a while.

Princess had a few hiccups before she was ready to run, like knocking the skin off her knee when she got cast in her stall one night, flailing about until the night watchman got her out of the corner, and after that she caught a case of the snots from some two year olds fresh off the farm which set her back another couple of weeks. So she didn't even make it to the races at Keeneland, but by the middle of June when they were back at Belmont again Ham reckoned she was as good as he could get her and he told J.B. so.

"The water's fine, boy, so you might as well jump right in," said J.B.

Proper Princess drew the rail in a maiden claimer going seven furlongs at Belmont and Johnny Mallano did everything he could to keep her there, saving all the ground and making one run to take the lead at the eighth pole, but the favorite got up the last few jumps and they had to settle for second.

Ham was disappointed that she didn't win but when he got back to the barn there was a cake that Hayley made and a party for him and when J.B. and Willie both told him he might be the best trainer they ever saw who hadn't yet had his eighteenth birthday, that picked his head right up.

Hayley roomed with another exercise girl named Barb who worked for what Willie said was one of the "blue-blood" outfits, those on the payroll for families with old money that went back to when their great-grandpa made the family fortune in railroads or steel or the oil business or maybe made uniforms for the Civil War.

Barb rode those blue-blood horses every day, sporting the same colors on her jacket and helmet cover as did the other five riders that worked for the outfit and she had to travel to the stakes races out of town so Hayley had the apartment to herself a lot and Ham got to hanging out there pretty regularly.

"That Kentucky woman works like a mule and looks after herself pretty good. Iffen' she could cook I'd be fighting you for her," said Willie.

"How do you know she can't?" said Ham and Willie just laughed.

It was the last Saturday in July when Ham and Willie took the train to Monmouth to watch a black filly named Ruffian that Hayley ponied when she won her first three outs by daylight and she was taking her to the post again in the Sorority Stakes.

Ruffian already had a reputation around the country and Frank Whitely had her running against a little peanut named Hot n Nasty that had broken her maiden by fourteen there at Monmouth and even shipped across the country to take a stakes race in California and Willie said if Ruffian could beat that speedball she might be another super horse like Big Red.

Hot n Nasty gave Ruffian a race though, and for the first time she felt the slap of a jockey's whip when Vasquez roused her to shake off the little one and boy oh boy said Willie, are you blest, Ham and Eggs, you get to see history in the making again.

Belmont Park was buzzing when the cops staged a raid early one morning, and Spider was the first one of the riders they led out in handcuffs. Detectives came around the barn once or twice, asking Ham some questions about Spider, probably the same questions they asked everyone who'd ever had anything to do with the little guy, as in did he ever talk about betting on the horses he rode or ask you to bet for him or did you ever see him with these guys, the toughs in the pictures they showed from the *New York Post* and the *Daily News*.

"They just fishin', so don't you go 'give them nothing to make something out of," said Willie, and that's what Ham did, he told them he knew Spider but not much else.

By the time the trial got started the races were back up-state at Saratoga and the story became daily grist for the backstretch rumor mill, everyone following the action in the *News* and the *Post* and having their own opinion on what would become of Spider and those nefarious gangsters.

Ham ran into Jake one morning, coming out of the track kitchen and they talked about Spider and how they all underestimated Spider when he and Ham walked in the barn at Saratoga on the same day.

"I thought he was an okay rider but I never figured him for a crook," said Jake, "but then again, I didn't think Nixon was one either."

He told Ham that the word on the backside was that Spider's old man had been a key player in the race-fixing operation, shipping in ringers from Argentina. They brought plain horses with no white socks or blazes that were easy to switch and they waited until they got a price before they ran the good ones and cashed big bets.

Since Spider was riding most of them he was in trouble up to his neck and the prosecutor wanted to paint him as one of the masterminds, looking like he was trying hard on horses that had no chance and sometimes they'd run the slow ones a couple of times before they switched. And it appeared that he and his father had been mixed up with those gangsters for a while, all the way back to when he started riding in Florida. He said they bet thousands and most of the money in Vegas so no one at the track would figure it out.

Ham had mixed feelings when the trial was over and Spider and his old man each got five years and he thought it stunk that the gangsters, those guys who'd probably made a ton of money, how they got away clean by making deals with the prosecutor and throwing Spider under the bus.

And he wondered where they would send Spider to prison and if he'd be able to go visit.

Proper Princess broke her maiden at the end of the Belmont meet but sure enough it was like Willie had told him when they got to Saratoga, it was "too tough" up there. Ham was happy enough when he had two seconds and a third in that company that almost added up to the same money as a win for a filly he'd bought for two grand.

And Princess might even have won the time she got beat three quarters of a length when the jock got stopped between horses in the stretch but Ham knew it was his own fault for keeping the tickets in his pants pocket and forgetting to stick them in his shirt pocket where they belonged.

While they were at Saratoga Ham took the bus up to Manchester to see his mom and the girls and he had planned to spend a couple of nights but quickly realized that one night was enough and he sure felt sorry for Steve being the only man in that old house with five women and only two bathrooms, but it explained a lot about him moving up in jobs at the resort, all the overtime he must have put in there.

Keeneland that October wasn't any easier for Proper Princess either, but Buster Brown put Ham in the winner's circle three more times in a row and the colt was getting talked about by the racing writers as if he might be the real deal.

When the reporter from the *Louisville Courier-Journal* was working on a story about J.B. she came by and asked Ham some questions and sure enough there was his name in the article.

After the outfit shipped back to Belmont, it seemed like their barn was as busy as a train station at rush hour and the boss put an end to all that when he set up sawhorses at the end of the shedrow to keep the reporters out and hired a second watchman to sit there during the daytime.

J.B. was abnormally taciturn but Willie said that was because it was the first time the man had his hands on a grade one horse and that would make anybody who smoked like he did burn up three packs a day.

They ran Buster in a couple of stakes races and it seemed the further they went, the better he liked it, breaking on top and almost rating himself on the lead with the jockey still like a silent passenger and when they almost won the Futurity, J.B. said that's enough, this bad boy is going to get a break and freshen up, it's a long way from now to the first Saturday in May.

On a chilly morning the week before Thanksgiving they were packing up the outfit to head south when a silver Mercedes two-seater with the top down pulled up to the barn and who was driving it but Lizzie, decked out in a fox fur jacket and designer jeans and tall boots and a jaunty cap, and she had two Springer spaniels in the back seat.

"Oo-oo-wee," said Willie, "Fanciest exercise girl I ever did see. Ham and Eggs, go put the saddle on one of those mustangs and give that girl a leg up."

"Sorry, Darlin," said Lizzie. "I'm retired."

And Willie told Ham see, I was right, our girl went off and found herself a rich man and Lizzie said damn right I did and he's a judge too so when you boys need to get out of jail just let me know, and that was good for a laugh.

Ham pulled Proper Princess out of her stall and was showing her off for Lizzie right when Hayley came around the corner and Willie saw it but Ham didn't as the two women eyed each other up and down and Hayley got a little red around her neck.

So Willie was quick to say c'mon with me Miss Lizzie and he took her down the shedrow to show her the other horses while Ham could pay attention to the right girl, the one who was there every day and never did try to push his buttons.

When Lizzie drove away Willie said:

"That old judge better be tied on for a helluva ride, hooking up with that little filly," meaning maybe that Lizzie would be a handful for whoever she was with and he told Ham he was lucky she was legal now or she might have put him in a jackpot, 'trying not to get sent back to England.

Ham turned eighteen back during the Saratoga meet and he had to register for the draft, but since they'd stopped calling soldiers up for military service the year before he never even had to take a physical.

Willie said that was something they had in common, not being in the military, since he'd been too young for World War I and too old for World War II but he said it made him proud when Ham told him he'd have served if he had been called but at the same time he was grateful that he'd been spared the experience. He told Ham that was a choice every man had to make for himself, like the great boxer Mohammed Ali, who gave up the best years of his career because of what he believed.

"When you look in that mirror every morning to shave, you 'got your own eyes looking back and there's no place to hide...'This above all else, to thine own self be true, and it must follow as the night the day, thou canst not be false to any man.'" said Willie, "That Shakespeare said a lot of things you can live by."

Ham told Willie how he'd heard some of Steve's stories from when he was a Ranger in Viet Nam and that killing someone seemed like the worst thing he could imagine having to do, but it maybe accounted for why the man was sometimes so quiet and distant, that he might be unable to forget some of those things he saw over there.

Willie didn't speak about his family much, but he did grow somber when they talked about the army and the wars, and said that every day he still missed his big brother that they lost in the first one and how it became his responsibility to help support those five sisters and a baby brother when his daddy got disabled with the bad heart that eventually took him to his maker.

Willie told Ham life's going to take you a lot of places,

"But if you 'need a good one to pass the time the Lord gave you, the racetrack is as good as any," he said, "with the same sun shining on everybody and for some it's as close to heaven as a man can get."

J.B. brought Buster Brown back to the track at Gulfstream in mid-December after the colt had a full month of rest at his farm in Kansas, and he said it was good they did because from here on they we're going to be playing in the big leagues.

A couple of weeks of galloping had gone by and it was time to start breezing and after Buster's first three-furlong work Ham thought the colt was a little off when he was cooling him out and told J.B. and right away the man called his vet and they jogged him on the road and sure enough Buster was nodding a touch, not lame, but still not perfect.

J.B. told Ham to go to the tack shop and get some Epsom salts and stop at the kitchen and get me a bacon, egg and cheese on a hard roll and Ham said he already had some salts in his wall box but J.B. said go on and do what you're told and when he got back the vet was gone and J.B. was walking Buster Brown and the colt was sound as a Yankee dollar.

A few days later Hayley galloped Buster and when the boss asked how'd he go she said he's hitting the ground okay but he doesn't seem like the same horse and the next day another exercise rider was on him.

Buster Brown made his next start as the big favorite in an allowance race at Gulfstream and got left flat-footed when the gate opened, but he had enough class to loop the field and still won by a couple of lengths.

That race was the first time he ran in his new silks, the black and white ones of a partner to whom J.B. had sold half the horses in his barn. He was some dentist from Atlanta that didn't practice anymore, just came to the track and made big bets and he claimed to have invented some special vitamins that made horses stay healthy.

They were all set to run Buster in the Hutcheson and after that the Fountain of Youth when he popped a quarter crack in his right front.

"That's all she wrote for the Derby," said Willie, but J.B. and his partner were determined to dance the big dance, so they flew in a blacksmith from Kentucky who knew how to put some wires and patches on the horse's foot and they ran him in the prep anyway.

"Damn fool way to treat a good horse," said Willie, "I don't know what's got into that man." But he said it quiet and just to Ham, not wanting to piss off his boss.

Buster Brown finished last and he didn't have to be vanned off, but the jock told them the colt was so sore he never tried a step and J.B. didn't have any choice but to put him away for the rest of the winter and that was the end of his Derby trail.

The dentist started showing up every morning and he filled more stalls with horses he bought at the two-year old sale and when he bought a piece of the rest of J.B.'s stock, right away the horses started running like trained pigs, and nothing in his silks finished worse than third for the rest of the winter.

J.B. was leading trainer after the first week at Belmont and the dentist leading owner and most of the ones they claimed won the first time they ran back, even if they were raised way up in class and looked hopeless.

And a month later the outfit had more wins than the next three stables put together until about ten-thirty one morning four black sedans parked at the ends of the shedrows and a dozen track security cops ran in the barn and told everybody stay right where you are while they searched the place.

Willie wasn't even there that day, gone home to Kentucky for his oldest sister's funeral, but when he got back J.B. told him to come in his office and close the door.

He told Willie the agents said they'd found a vial containing illegal drugs in a wall box and it had Willie's fingerprints all over it.

"That the same bottle you told me was vitamins? 'What the vet had left by mistake, and put them my box 'til the vet come back?" said Willie.

But J.B. said he better not say that to the stewards, because he'd have to deny it and then it would just be his word against Willie's and besides, Willie was the assistant trainer.

And J.B. told Willie that some people were out to get him because they were jealous of his success and it was a bad situation all around but he worked it out and Willie would take the blame this one time because too much depended on a boss for him to be suspended and Willie should just take the time off like a vacation and he'd double his pay, like a bonus while he was away, that was the deal.

"What kind of deal is that?" said Ham.

"Devil's deal, I reckon," said Willie, and Ham could see the hurt in his friend's eyes.

Ham rode the train to Grand Central Station with Willie and they walked to the Port Authority so he could he could catch his bus back home to Kentucky.

"It's just not right," said Ham, and he needed a handkerchief to wipe his eyes.

"Take care of yourself, and be careful who you put your trust in," said Willie and Ham watched an older Willie than he'd ever seen climb onto that bus.

Ham stuck around for a couple of weeks, living alone in the tack room and taking care of Buster Brown who wasn't nearly the same horse he'd been, no matter what vitamins the dentist fed him.

The stable had gone cold and hadn't run a winner since Willie left and one day J.B. snapped and swore at Ham for no good reason, using words that insulted his mother and Ham said sorry sir but I'm not a dog and I'll not be working here anymore and J.B. told him to pack his gear and get the hell out and take that grey mare with you.

Ham didn't have much time to think over what he might do, but he was headed to the track kitchen for a coffee and a quiet moment when he ran into Hayley and told her what had happened. She said one of the pony riders had an empty stall and they'll let you keep Princess there until you come up with another job and that's what he did.

Word travels fast on the backstretch and before noon Ham already had a couple of job offers, but he didn't think he wanted to go to work for any of them, those guys who had a barn full and wanted you to rub four horses that might be there one day and gone the next.

Those were what Willie called "livery stables," that ran like a production line and treated the horses like machines, claiming and dropping, claiming and dropping or buying young horses from the sales by the dozen and running them until they fell apart.

Tony the van driver knew just about everybody and just about everybody's business and Tony told Ham that he had friends with a nice farm that they could send Princess to for a lay-up and the people would take good care of her and not charge him too much while Ham got to figure out what he'd do next.

CHAPTER 11

1975-76

Never a day went by that Ham didn't think about what happened to Willie and try to figure out where everything went wrong.

He knew there wasn't a more honest soul walking the backstretch and yet there was Willie, marked forevermore as a cheating horse-drugger while the guilty one was free to carry on as if nothing had happened.

So it wasn't long before J.B. got himself in trouble again and tried to make another deal so he could keep training for the dentist, but the cops were watching him and his barn got a shake down almost every week and eventually he disappeared, probably back to that farm in Kansas.

After a couple of months of doing catch-work for a few trainers he liked but not wanting to commit to any full-time job, Ham decided to get his trainer's license and take

Hayley up on her idea to go to Monmouth Park for the summer. Hayley had been married a while back to a Jersey trainer and spent a few summers there with him so she knew her way around that neck of the woods.

Ham brought Proper Princess and Hayley owned two geldings that ran mostly in starter handicaps and seemed to always pay their way and she said her Dad would put up some money for them to claim a couple more.

Ham rubbed the horses and trained them and she galloped them all and rubbed some herself and they got a place to live over in West End near the beach, the top floor of an old Victorian house that had been chopped up into a bunch of apartments and theirs was only two rooms with a tiny kitchen and there were huge oak trees on the property, so they didn't ever need air conditioning no matter how hot and humid it got.

Ham said he was hoping Willie could come and be with them when he got done serving his suspension, but when he called and talked to him about it Willie said I don't know son I think I'm too tired and maybe I'm done with the track and that upset Ham to no end.

He asked Tony to let him know when the next van was going to Kentucky and when it was he told Hayley he had to go take care of some business and she knew he was going to see Willie.

"Sixty years might be enough," said Willie.

"But it's what you love, 'being with those racehorses, and besides, we need you," said Ham, but Willie wouldn't get out of his rocking chair on the porch of the old grey stone house that generations his family had lived in for almost a hundred years and Ham noticed that the sprinkle of white across Willie's temples had spread over his head, almost as if he'd been out in a snowstorm.

"I'll always be with you, Ham and Eggs," said Willie, touching his heart, "And you with me, son."

Ham knew he wouldn't convince Willie to come with him right then, so when he finally got the old man to say I'll think about it and maybe I might see you later, Ham took that as good enough and set out that very afternoon, hitch-hiking back on the same path he'd just taken across the Alleghenies and the Blue Ridge Mountains.

Ham and Hayley had two horses in on that Saturday, but he still had the little black and white TV that he and Willie used to watch races when they couldn't get away from the barn, so when the match race between Ruffian and Foolish Pleasure came on they were able to take a time-out.

"Speed horse always wins a match race," said Ham, echoing an old Willie-adage, "'cause if they get to the front and make their own pace, if they're any good at all, the closer can't get by."

As the two horses leapt free at the start, Ruffian hit her shoulder on the gate leaving there and Foolish Pleasure grabbed the lead for a few strides, but the black filly blazed to the front and after a quarter mile she was in control.

Hayley gasped when Vasquez had to struggle to pull Ruffian up, his hands full with her still wanting to run, and no one watching the race needed an announcer to tell them she'd broken down.

Hayley's knees buckled and it was lucky that Ham was right next to her to catch her as she fainted.

Ham and Hayley worked like demons that summer and when Hayley's Jersey-bred gelding won by a few lengths, Ham made a smart-aleck remark about it being an easy game and he knew right away he shouldn't have said that, because for the next five starts their horses didn't even get a check.

But they kept at it and by the time Labor Day rolled around they had three more winners to show for their efforts and he wished he'd bet on a couple of the ones that paid big prices but money was tight and without Willie around he wasn't that game anymore.

It seemed that the extra money all went to the feed man and the vet and the blacksmith and the tooth man and much as he would have liked to put them off, Ham couldn't bring himself to being known as another guy who didn't pay his bills.

Ham and Hayley were hanging out on the boardwalk in Long Branch after a hot dog supper at Max's, amusing themselves by watching the tourists that the locals called Bennys when a small man in a dark suit and shiny black shoes strolled up and respectfully addressed them as Mister and Missus Greer and said he was sorry to interrupt but could he please have a moment of their time.

Hayley giggled at the Mister and Missus part, but she stayed quiet after Ham didn't bother to correct the man and tell him no they weren't married, but just stood and shook hands and said yessir, how are you and what can we do for you.

He said he'd bet on Proper Princess and a couple of their other winners and the thought their horses stood out in the walking ring.

"I've always wanted to have some Thoroughbreds," said the man, "and now I'm going to get some and have you train them. What do you think of that?"

He said he'd treat the racehorse game just like he did his other business and maybe they'd have some luck, which of course were two different things, but not to his way of thinking.

"Sounds fine to me," said Ham after deferring for a moment to Hayley who said it sounded fine to her too and I think you've made a wise decision sir, this guy is going to be a great horse trainer.

Mister Adams' wife liked to kid and say he even wore a suit to bed, but it may have been true, because when he came to the barn that was the way he always dressed, dark blue or black jacket and pants and a white shirt but never a tie.

Missus Adams didn't come around the stables at first but when they bought a package deal of horses from the mid-west and filled a whole side of a barn at Atlantic City Race Course, she jumped right in and brought a landscaper with a truck full of shrubs and flowers.

And she set to designing the jockey silks, a pale shade of blue with yellow polka dots and a blue cap and they got wall plaques made and then t-shirts and caps for all the grooms and an expensive blue suede jacket for Ham.

Missus Adams took Hayley shopping with her and Ham kidded that "Missus Greer" was starting to look like a fashion model and he hoped he didn't have to find another exercise girl.

The first few of the Adams' horses didn't run that well because Ham ran them in tough spots since he was a little anxious starting out with somebody else's money, but by the end of the meet they had themselves a few trophies and Missus Adams started a wall of winner's photos in the den.

Ham took the money he made and reinvested it in dressing his barn properly and bought all new buckets and feed tubs and new rakes and pitchforks and wheelbarrows.

When Mister Adams took Ham to Keeneland for the fall yearling sale Hayley stayed behind and looked after the barn and Ham fell back on what he'd learned in Florida, working for the vet at the Hialeah sales to look for a good horse.

They flew there on the Adams' private jet and they would only have bought two or three if it were up to Ham, but Mister Adams got caught up in the competition of bidding and signed for a half-a-dozen yearlings and the bill ran over two hundred thousand but the man never blinked an eye.

The stable just starting to get rolling at Garden State with a winner the first weekend, and that became Ham's game plan, to get in what Willie called a "Saturday horse" when the owners would come with a bunch of their friends in tow.

The filly that won was a roan two year old that they'd found at a local sale and paid next to nothing for compared to the money Mister Adams shelled out for those Kentucky yearlings and he'd named her Rebecca's Rose after their ten year old daughter. They brought the girl and her friends to the barn on weekend mornings to feed carrots to all their horses, but "Rosie" became one of the family.

"I want to take her home and keep her in my room," said Rebecca, and her father laughed.

Ham called Kentucky every day for a week, trying to talk with Willie and he made plans to take a plane there when one morning a woman answered the phone. It was Willie's sister, the last of his siblings, and she told Ham that Willie was in the hospital but he'd probably be okay and that he'd said to tell him so.

Ham talked it over with Hayley and they decided that for his own peace of mind that he'd better fly there and see for himself and the next morning he did just that.

"Diabetes," said Willie, "Making my eyesight worse is all, but I feel fine otherwise."

And Willie told Ham he might try to come back east to help him and Hayley when winter arrived and make sure you keep that tack room for me with an extra cot in it in case that Kentucky woman kicks you out and you need a place to sleep but Ham had a feeling it was a longshot he'd ever show up.

Ham's plane to Philadelphia didn't leave Louisville until noon, so he wasn't there when Hayley took Rebecca's Rose to the paddock for the stakes race, but she outshone the other horses and Rebecca's friends squealed like only little girls can when the filly wheeled and bucked, just feeling so good.

The horses were bunched on the turn when the filly inside Rebecca's Rose clipped the heels of the one in front of her and took a nosedive and there was no way for Rosie to avoid her.

"Oh, God," whispered Hayley.

"What happened?" said everyone else.

Hayley left the Adams' and their friends in the box seats and ran all the way to the quarter pole but the green screen was up and the vet already had the syringe out when she got there. The filly had broken her shoulder, tripping over the fallen horse.

Hayley stood quietly and watched Ham at his desk in the tack room office.

"Yessir," said Ham, "Yessir, I understand."

Ham hung up the phone and held his head in his hands.

"He quit," said Ham.

"Quit?" said Hayley.

"'Said he was sorry, but Rebecca still hasn't stopped crying... he just called a bloodstock agent and he's sold all the horses..."

"It wasn't anybody's fault, it was an accident," said Hayley.

"He knows that," said Ham.

When Ham called Willie to tell him what happened Willie told him the Lord works in mysterious ways and Ham said if that's how He works count me out and a few other things he regretted afterward having said to his old friend.

Ham and Hayley packed up the three horses they'd started with and her pony and shipped them to Tampa Bay Downs the week before Thanksgiving and neither went home for the holiday although they talked about it but decided they couldn't afford to, not knowing how long the money Adams gave them would have to last. They got a motel room near the track and drove Hayley's pickup truck back and forth to work.

They had four stalls in the middle of a barn with a bunch of other ragtag outfits in the same boat, either family shoe-string operations or a single person with one or two horses and in one of their stalls they kept Hayley's pony.

Jake was there too at the other side of the barn, doing most of the work for an old man who only had a couple of horses and he said being broke wasn't so bad if you didn't have to take orders, and he'd ask Ham to join him in a beer at the end of the day and once in a while he did while they watched the sun go down over the racetrack.

"That pony took Ruffian to the post," Hayley told the neighbors in the barn. And she got some work that made her a few bucks here and there, ponying those horses that were too sore to have a rider on their back every day.

The couple at the end of the barn fought incessantly and one morning Ham had to step in when the guy backhanded his girlfriend right there in the shedrow.

"Mind your own business," said the guy and he backed off but it wasn't long before he did it again and somebody complained and the cops came and took him away in handcuffs. Hayley helped the girl take care of their horses, but she about went crazy when the girl bailed her abuser out and a day later there he was again, yelling at her and shoving her around.

After that Ham and Hayley kept to themselves and when a Canadian trainer claimed both of Hayley's geldings they didn't know whether to count themselves lucky or not. The horses hadn't won a race for a while and they were trying to run them where they thought they had a chance but neither had hit the board so they had to feel like it was a good thing, two less mouths to feed. Ham put Proper Princess in a claimer for ten thousand and damned if the guy didn't try to take her too, but he made a spelling mistake and his claim slip was voided.

By the time they finished paying their bills they just under ten thousand left and Hayley told Ham they'd been together long enough just getting by and for a week she cried about wanting them to get married. At one point he almost weakened and said sure, but then he called Willie to talk it over.

"Don't do nothing your heart don't tell you is right," said Willie, "but if it does, then go on and do it."

When Ham told Hayley he needed to think on it a bit, she didn't say much but when he stayed at the barn put a poultice on Proper Princess she went back to the motel, packed up and took half of the money and when he walked back from the track he found the note she left him tacked on the door.

The note said:

Good Bye and Good Luck Hamilton Greer. I've had enough of living like a gypsy.

Love, H.

Ham was staying in the tack room and taking care of Princess when Jake asked him if he could use the other stall that was still empty for a two year old colt he found at a farm in Ocala and gave five thousand for and if Ham wanted to, he could be in for half. Ham said sure, 'might as well take a shot, 'cause like Willie said, if a peanut farmer from Georgia can get to be President of the United States, a kid from Vermont might train a Derby winner some day.

He figured he'd have to find a job rubbing horses for somebody in a couple of weeks anyway when the track closed and he and Jake would both be down to case cash, but a week later Jake announced he needed to go back to Vermont and give me a thousand and you can have my half, pay me the rest on the cuff if he makes you any money.

Tony the van man did Ham a favor and gave him and his two horses a free ride to Calder and the barn they ended up in was at the back of the stable area and had more mosquitoes than the Amazon jungle until an early tropical storm blew through and cleaned the air.

Ham didn't speak any Spanish and he was at the end of the shedrow from a couple of Cubans who didn't know English very well, so it was like being cloistered for a couple of weeks until a free-lance exercise boy from Trinidad named Cecil started coming around and he had somebody to talk to in the mornings.

Proper Princess fit well with the Calder summer horses and she could have won all three of the starter handicaps if her rider hadn't eased up right before the wire and got her beat a nose in the last one.

Ham thought about claiming another but he knew he was better off with a two horse stable with ones that could run than he was having a bunch of slow ones that needed the runners to carry their bills.

The big black colt he got from Jake was already named Snuggler and Cecil had trouble saying that so he'd show up and ask is "Zuggler" ready. They galloped him for three weeks and on a quiet Monday Ham said just turn him loose a little through the lane and let's see what happens.

Ham watched from the open stands and the clocker turned to him and said,

"Who the hell is that?"

"Two year old," said Ham.

There was no one else in the boxes or on the apron below.

"That there is a runner," said the clocker.

In New York Seattle Slew was breaking everybody's watch when he worked, so it was no surprise when he went to the post as favorite in his first start, and again in his second and in his third when Ham and Cecil watched him gallop home a winner in the Champagne Stakes and Cecil pointed at the TV and said:

"He looks just like Zuggler."

Snuggler was almost ready to run when he was feeling so good that he reared up and hit the front of his head on the crossbeam overhead of the stall door and needed a dozen stitches. It wasn't serious but sure looked ugly so Ham passed the first maiden race and on the second Saturday in November he entered him and walked the black colt to the paddock with Cecil alongside to help.

As the starting gate sprung open Snuggler broke a step slow, but he had a good post position in the middle of a small field and when Gene St. Leon swung him to the three-path at the top of the stretch, he drew off without a single touch of the whip.

Ham called Willie that night and for the first time in a while he heard some strength in the old man's voice. Willie said he was sorry he couldn't be there but God bless you son and when Ham said he'd send Willie a plane ticket if he'd come to Florida and take the winter in some warm sunshine, Willie said he'd like that but not right now thanks.

Ham hadn't kept up with his running after Hayley left and when he went to Calder it was too hot and he had so much work to do that the only thing he wanted to do in the afternoons was take a nap.

But after the black colt started off so well he thought maybe that was a sign for him to get himself going and move his blood around. It was just about a mile around on the turf course if he ran the outside of the track, so he made it his business to do least two laps in the evening, sometimes even three or four before he went to supper.

He was dragging himself back to the barn one evening when a car stopped to let him pass and it was Bogie, waving him over.

"Hey kid, how you doing?" said Bogie.

"Better than a lot of folks I guess," said Ham.

And Bogie told him he was working as a jockey agent now, carrying the book of a Chicago rider named Snyder who probably wouldn't get many mounts there but wanted to try a winter in the sun.

"Honest as hell, too," said Bogie and how about putting him on that two year old that just won for fun.

"I think Gene would feed me to one of those circus lions," said Ham, "But if anything happens I'll sure look for you."

Ham was getting a lot of advice what to do next with Snuggler, so he called Willie and Willie's sister said he was sleeping, could you call back and she didn't know that Ham wasn't aware of it when she told him Willie was having a tough time with not being able to see anymore.

He told her not to let on that he knew and he'd call back tomorrow noon and went right to the tack room to spill some tears for his best friend.

When Willie answered he sounded in good spirits and they talked about the black colt and decided that they'd treat him like he might be a good one and they'd put him in an allowance race for non-winners of two lifetime at a mile and not throw him to the wolves in a stakes race like everybody else wanted.

St. Leon let Snuggler settle back in the pack going into the first turn and get some dirt in his face just to see what he'd do and the colt didn't like it at all and just dropped back to last before they straightened down the backstretch.

"Shoot," said Ham.

"It's okay," said Cecil, and by the time they passed the three-eighths pole the jock had Snuggler three-wide and he had passed half the field and was gaining on the leaders. He only won by a head, but when St. Leon came back he told Ham it was never in doubt and buddy you got yourself a runner there.

The next day Ham went to the bank and got a money order for five thousand dollars and sent it to Jake in Vermont. Jake called the stable gate and left a message and Ham called him back.

"That's more than you owe me," said Jake.

"He's a good horse," said Ham, "You should buy your half back. You can have it for what you sold it to me."

"Nah, a deal's a deal," said Jake, "But you're a good man, Greer."

The racing reporter for the *Miami Herald* came by the barn next morning and he followed Ham around the walking ring as he gave Snuggler a day off from the track, asking him questions the whole time and taking notes as they walked.

The article he wrote said Ham was from Kentucky but that was the only mistake and since Ham spoke mostly about Willie and with him being in Kentucky that was understandable.

Ham cut the article out of the paper and stuck it in an envelope and sent it to his mom in a Christmas card with a hundred dollar bill, like he'd been doing for the past few years.

When he called her on Christmas Eve he talked about his plans with Snuggler and where he would go after Florida and when she asked about that pretty girl Hayley he'd told her about, he said it hadn't worked out but he was okay and he was just going to wait by the bus stop until another one came by.

CHAPTER 12

1977-78

"You 'better off to be a big fish in a small pond than to get yourself 'et up being a little one in a race that's too tough," said Willie, "'cause it's better to win a small one than run for second when you can't beat somebody 'cause you still got to beat the other ones anyway."

Ham knew Willie was right, that he should stay there at Calder with Snuggler but when it came time to make a decision he started doing an extra lap around the turf track, trying to figure out every possibility of what could happen. He was just about ready to run the colt in an allowance race when the *Miami Herald* printed another story speculating about him shipping out for a little stakes race at Tampa Bay, something he'd not even considered before he saw it in print.

After folks read that Hamilton Greer wasn't even twenty-one yet and training a colt that the writer said was the biggest sleeper horse he'd ever seen for the Kentucky

Derby, Ham started thinking maybe this was his big chance and what if Snuggler was a big-time horse, wouldn't he be missing the boat.

He began to get phone calls and notes and even visits at the barn from folks who said they wanted to talk with him about taking their horses, but in fact most were really only interested in hearing the sound of their own bragging.

Bloodstock agents wore a path to the barn every day with a new deal to buy Snuggler and that led to Ham taking a drink or two with Cecil in the afternoon thinking it might calm his nerves, but sometimes the drinks carried on into the evening and that only made the next morning tougher.

He kept going to the pay phone by the track kitchen, trying to call Willie but there was no answer in Kentucky.

When the offer finally got over a hundred-fifty thousand dollars for a horse that cost five, he thought it was too much to pass and Ham shook on the deal but the x-rays showed a small chip in the colt's ankle. The buyer walked away and pretty soon word got around that Snuggler wouldn't pass the vet and there weren't any more offers of real money, just "if-come" propositions, so Ham got to thinking about the Tampa race and the chance for some good money there.

He'd had to skip a couple of workouts while the dickering went on and when they went to Tampa the colt drew the far outside post position in a full field but the *Herald* writer picked him to win anyway.

"Scratch that sonofagun," said Willie when Ham finally got him on the phone.

By the time the thunderstorm ceased the horses had been waiting in the paddock for an extra half hour and humidity rose from the ground like steam off hot stones in a sauna bath and half of them were sweating so much that they looked like they'd already run.

St. Leon was obligated to ride the favorite so Ham gave the mount on Snuggler to Bogie's rider and before he gave him a leg up, he told the jock to try and get some position early on and maybe he could get behind a couple of early runners in a speed duel.

The riders circled their mounts behind the gate and Ham got as close on the outside fence as he could to the start and watched Snyder use his stick to wipe the white foam off Snuggler's neck and shoulder.

St. Leon gunned his little chestnut to the lead as soon as the latch sprung and before the horses made the Clubhouse turn he had a comfortable lead on his own. Snuggler got hung out to dry from his outside post, not being able to drop in behind the others, and Ham reckoned he lost about five lengths just being stuck out there and if he hadn't he would have won instead of finishing fifth like he did.

Ham could see the scribe from the *Miami Herald* interviewing the winning trainer as he sponged some cold water over Snuggler's brow and wondered if the man would come by but he never did.

The colt checked out real well and was none the worse for the race except for a pretty good crease down his back from getting so tired and being a little pissed off from all the mud he got splashed back in his face.

It was a full week later before Ham got up the courage to call Willie. He knew Willie wasn't one to berate, but he also knew he deserved a proper ass-kicking for not listening when he knew damn well it wasn't the right thing to run a good horse short on training into a stakes race and that guilt made him keep calling until he finally got the old man on the phone.

"Did you see the race?" said Ham, a stupid question to ask a blind person.

"Wasn't much to see from what I heard," said Willie.

"I'm sorry, I should have listened to you, but..."

"If ifs and buts was candy and nuts, then everyday be Christmas, 'the way I see it," said Willie, and Ham smiled at hearing a familiar homily.

"You got any money left, son?"

"Got a few bucks, I'm okay," said Ham.

"Remember what I told you, son, if you do the right thing by your horse, 'you do the right thing for yourself."

"Yessir," said Ham.

When Proper Princess bowed a tendon in her next start and finished last, that might have been disastrous and Ham was beginning to think maybe his luck couldn't get any worse, but then he considered it might be changing when the Canadian who claimed her managed to fill out the slip the right way this time. And Ham didn't feel bad at all about the man getting a horse that couldn't run anymore when the guy told him he'd taken her to be a broodmare and her racing days were over anyway.

Ham used his claim money from Princess to pay off the feed man and the vet and he paid a thousand in advance on the farm bill where he'd sent Snuggler for his layup. With the rest of the money he bought a plane ticket to LaGuardia and hitchhiked from there up the Henry Hudson Parkway to Albany, then took Rt. 7 on home to Vermont.

He hadn't told his mother he was coming, since he didn't want to explain his situation turning dire after so much bragging in his letters with the newspaper articles he'd sent her.

So it was a big surprise to Ham when he got to Manchester and no one was there, just a for-sale sign on the front lawn and an empty house to greet him. He went down the lane and knocked on his Aunt Helen's door, the one that was his mother's oldest sister and had always called him Dolly ever since he was a baby when she thought he was cute as a doll.

Aunt Helen told him come on in Dolly and have something to eat with us and she told him about Steve's new job up in Stowe at the Trapp Family Lodge and said he had better stay in their spare room until he was ready to move on.

It had been twenty-five years between Citation and Secretariat without a Triple Crown, so racing folks were giddy with the prospect of another so soon and on top of that, Seattle Slew was undefeated.

Ham watched Slew's Derby and Preakness and Belmont from another tack room, this one in Middleburg, Virginia.

Tony the van man's brother Vince worked at the Mellon estate as part of the staff at the big house and he lived in a small cottage on the grounds. He let Ham stay in his spare room until he got a job over at Mister Mellon's private training center, and when Snuggler arrived from Ocala half-a-hand taller, the manager had already heard all about the kid trainer and said he called in a favor and it was okay for Ham keep his horse there while he rubbed four of the Rokeby blue-bloods.

Some of the stable hands at the training center had been around for two decades and had their hands on plenty of good horses for Mister Mellon and the other tall man who trained for him, Elliott Burch.

The office was a simple room, halters and bridles and saddles all about but the winners circle pictures of Arts and Letters and Fort Marcy caught Ham's eye as soon as he entered. A little gnome of a man they called Scooter who walked hots told him stories about how he helped break those two champions and plenty of the other Rokeby stakes winners.

Scooter barely came up to Ham's elbow and he'd been a jockey back in his day in the '40s and it seemed he hadn't forgotten a moment of the decades he spent on the track. He used a lot of the same expressions that Willie did and it made Ham homesick for his days in the tackroom with that other old man and when Scooter told Ham he was going down to the Inn for a pop, Ham knew he wasn't talking about Coca Cola so he went along and nursed a beer while he listened to more tales.

Ham had his colt legged up pretty well at the training center and when Scooter gifted Ham a recycled Rokeby halter that he said was once worn by Key to the Mint the old man joked that Snuggler looked like new money.

With one horse and only a few hundred left in his kick, Saratoga wasn't in Ham's future so he took Willie's advice and called the Racing Secretary at Penn National and gave him a story about maybe having another horse coming from the farm and they gave him two stalls although if they'd said one Ham would have taken that.

Harrisburg, Pennsylvania felt like light years away from places like Saratoga and Hialeah and Belmont, but Ham's chest swelled a bit right away when the first exercise boy galloped Snuggler and the kid they called Duck for his '50s haircut jumped off the big black colt.

"Runnin' sonofabitch, that one," said Duck, who had sat on plenty of good horses and knew one when he saw it. They breezed Snuggler a few times short and then one morning Ham told Duck to let him roll a half.

The clocker caught Smug galloping out in a minute flat and told Ham that Buck Thornburg was coming to ride in the Governor's Cup for Del Carroll and here's his agent's number, tell him I said to call.

The horse Thornburg came to ride didn't hit the board and the jock was known for being a man of few words, but after they took the winners circle picture on Snuggler he slid out of the saddle and told Ham to walk this way kid.

"Wherever and whenever that horse runs back, I'm riding him," he said.

Three weeks later Ham put Snuggler in a little stakes race and once again after the winners circle ceremony Thornburg said the very same thing. They ran off a string of three wins and each time after the race Ham would call Willie and Willie would tell him to thank the Lord and stay in that little pond.

Ham thought about getting an apartment, but he'd been there two months and still only had the one horse so he bought a used pickup truck and a trailer with the money Snuggler had won for him, figuring he might try hauling him to Keeneland and that way he'd get to see Willie again.

He knew what Willie would say if he asked about running at Keeneland, that he was getting to big for his britches but he'd gotten hold of a condition book and found a race there that could only be too tough if there was a big-time horse in it coming off a rest and he reckoned Snuggler was dead-fit and he'd be the one to beat anyway.

When he called to tell Willie he was coming, Willie's sister said he'd been under the weather and didn't feel like talking on the phone but he would like Ham to come by on the weekend and make sure you call before you come, just in case.

The stall Keeneland gave Ham was in an old barn at the top of the hill, way in the back of the stable area and a long hike to the main track, but he had a tack room to sleep in so the first day there he walked Snuggler and took a long nap and the second morning he was going to look for a free-lance exercise rider when Hayley showed up.

"I thought you abandoned the gypsy life," said Ham.

"I'm respectable now three days a week, helping out at the vet clinic over in Harrodsburg," she said, "And 'got this too," flashing a diamond engagement ring.

He gave her a leg up on Snuggler and walked them to the training track and told her to back him up to the wire and jog twice around and it was all she could do to pull him up at the outside fence.

"I'm no lion-tamer," she said, "You better take this guy out and let him do something tomorrow or Superman won't be able to hold him."

Next morning they went at dawn, first ones to step on the main track.

"Let him think he's running off with you, he likes that," said Ham, "then get down the last eighth and really let him open his lungs."

Willie answered the phone on the first ring and Ham felt a lift at hearing the energy in the old man's voice.

"Maybe you might ought to come by and we can have us a talk," said Willie.

"I'll be there in half an hour," said Ham and he asked the guy at the end of the barn to keep an eye on Snuggler while he went out for a bit.

The old stone house was just as Ham remembered it, except for the freshly painted shutters. Willie was sitting on the porch in a rocking chair and didn't seem to notice when Ham parked his truck in the driveway and Ham thought he might be sleeping.

He skipped a couple of the front steps on the way up and Willie said:

"That you, boy?"

"I'm glad to see you," said Ham.

Willie was wearing dark glasses and he stood with the help of a cane and didn't look right at Ham, just in his general direction.

"I'd be glad to see anything, but that's not the way the Good Lord wants it," said Willie.

And it only took a few days for the folks in the barn to get used to that sight, a blind man leading a big black horse, the same horse they were used to seeing prance around and rear up on his hind legs, but with that old man he behaved like a pony at a petting zoo.

It seemed that Willie didn't need his sight to be around horses, and from the first time he told Ham to give him the shank he'd walk over to Snuggler and Snuggler would cozy right up to Willie and he strolled next to him like a pussycat, not pulling or dragging him like he did every other hotwalker he ever had except Ham.

Hayley started crying when she saw Willie, not just because of his being blind, but because she was flooded with memories from their days back east when he gave her a job galloping and she first met Ham.

Willie acted like Willie always did; taking a situation that might make lots of folks give up what made them happy, but not him, taking in the sounds and smells of the barn as

he just moved slower and spoke more softly, content to know that what he said was being listened to by ones he loved.

The day before Snuggler was entered to run, a gold Rolls Royce pulled up to the barn and the chauffeur held the door open for a blonde lady in a pink Chanel suit.

Ham and Willie were sitting in a pair of worn out easy chairs at the end of the shedrow outside the tack room where they slept.

"I'm looking for Mister Greer the trainer," said the lady, and she looked Ham up and down when he said yes Ma'am that would be me.

"I guess I was expecting someone older," she said.

"He's old but he'd had an easy life," said Willie and she looked at him like she wasn't sure what to make of the old man in the dark glasses.

She told Ham she wanted to buy Snuggler if he could run in her silks and when he told her he wouldn't pass the vet she said she didn't care, she'd just lease him for the day, she had friends coming to the races that afternoon and she was sure he'd win and she wanted to take them to the winners circle to have their picture taken.

Willie laughed out loud when she said that but she paid him no mind, just took out her check book and wrote a check for ten thousand dollars and said they could spilt the purse and Ham talked it over with Willie who said don't be stupid, if she wants to give that much go on and take it.

Ham told Willie Missus Joplin had nine friends with her in the winner's circle and he guessed a thousand a head was what she wanted to pay for a picture with them.

"Come up to the Turf Club, dah-ling," said Missus Joplin after the race and please, Missus Joplin was my mother, you can call me Pamela.

Ham told her he had to get back to the barn and she said she'd bring her entourage over to see her horse after they'd had some champagne. .

Ham had Snuggler bathed and done up by the time they showed up in the Rolls and before she left she told Ham she'd send her car to bring him to dinner and he finally gave in and said okay.

"Be careful," was all Willie said but Ham didn't think it was bad, all the attention he was getting and riding in the Rolls Royce and dining at a restaurant that had white tablecloths and cloth napkins, where the waiter kept your wine glass full.

Ham wouldn't sell Snuggler to Pamela but he agreed she could lease him whenever she liked and for the next week she came to the barn every day with a bloodstock agent and at least one new horse she'd bought for Ham to train.

The Racing Secretary moved the other trainers out and gave Ham the rest of the barn and pretty soon there were twenty-five new heads poking out of those stalls.

Pamela was talking about having another dozen when they got to Florida, but they'd have to stable at Gulfstream because it's too long a drive from where she lives in Palm Beach and besides, she heard that Hialeah is in a bad neighborhood, no matter how nice Ham said it was.

She said she'd like to get a horse like Affirmed or maybe Alydar and maybe Affirmed would be champion two year old this year but she was sure that Alydar would be the better of the pair when they turned three and went for the Derby and it wouldn't surprise her if there was another Triple Crown winner, two in a row.

Willie brought around some barn help that he trusted, guys named Bugs and Dirt and Heavy to rub the horses and Heavy's girl friend Little Star who had a gold tooth in front with a diamond in it to fill the hotwalker's job.

They weren't much to look at, but Ham knew Willie wouldn't bring anybody he didn't trust and soon the Keeneland barn was just like Bogie's old barn at Hialeah, Willie cooking southern and Little Star keeping the place like a palace.

Everyone called Pamela "Boss-Lady" whenever she came around and the time she brought Champagne to the barn and got everyone drunk they all called her "Pam-Pam" and she loved it.

The last week of the Keeneland meet Snuggler won another allowance race but the ankle with the chip was warm afterwards and Willie said let's get an ex-ray of that and if it's not too bad we can send this big boy to the farm for a blister and a rest and maybe he'll be back at Hialeah when we need him.

Ham and Pamela were alone on the restaurant patio in Lexington where you could still eat outside on a warm fall evening. The other diners were gone and she'd had more than a few glasses of Moet when she took his hand and looked in his eyes and told him she was "fond" of him.

Ham didn't know exactly how old she was, but he reckoned she was almost his mom's age and he wasn't exactly sure how to feel about that "fondness."

She told him she felt a little light-headed from too much bubbly and maybe he could help her back to her suite at the hotel and when they got there it was pretty clear what else she wanted him to do.

Ham made it to the barn by six the next morning, and Willie already had the first set out and was giving Hayley a leg up on one of the new horses, the most expensive one the lady had bought for over a hundred grand.

Willie said maybe you should watch this colt, son, the riders say he climbs and I put a shadow roll on him to see if he'd level out.

They were in Pamela's box seats at Keeneland when the new horse passed, giving Hayley all she could handle and Ham described to Willie what he saw, how the colt was throwing his head from side to side.

"Dang," said Willie, "Wasn't the shadows, it's his mouth," and Ham said how come you're a blind man and you see things people with two good eyes can't see.

When they got the colt back to the barn Willie made Ham put his fingers in the horses' mouth and said feel this boy, that's what you call a wolf tooth, what's been bugging him.

And Ham waited all morning for Willie to say something about Missus Joplin and him being gone all night but he never said a word.

For a man who'd just lost his sight, Willie got along pretty well but he said that was because it took so long coming that he'd had a chance to get used to darkness.

He didn't use the white cane around the barn for fear it would upset the horses, but he said he knew the shedrow in his mind like it was his mama's face and if you watched him move about, one might not even suspect he was blind.

And the few folks in the backstretch that didn't love him before all came to be fascinated by the old man tapping his way to the kitchen, grabbing a tray and picking his food as he made his way through the line.

Blondie the cashier always gave him more back in change than what he paid but Willie quickly figured that out and he got a kick out of it so he let her do it and once a week he'd bring her a box of the saltwater taffy that she told him she liked from when she worked at the Atlantic City track.

Willie told Ham he'd go to Florida with him but maybe Ham should get a proper place to stay, not bunking down with an old man and they argued a bit about that, Ham saying he wouldn't sleep right worrying until finally Willie said okay, now you're the boss.

Ham walked Snuggler off the van at Gulfstream and the black colt nickered from the minute he snapped the shank on his halter.

"He missed you," said Willie.

"He's my Delilah," said Ham and Willie said then you better sing to him, they always run better when you do.

Ham walked the colt for a few days before they started jogging him and Willie said that ankle feels cold as ice and maybe we might have some fun with him after all.

Ham's plan was to get Snuggler ready for the Donn Handicap and Willie said we might as well aim high now, we're back in the big pond and besides, that lady with all the money likes to have the cameras pointed in her direction.

Missus Joplin didn't show up at the barn very often, but once in a while the Rolls would pull up and she'd have a few fancy people in tow, maybe they'd been out all night and hadn't even been home yet, coming right from the bars and the parties.

She didn't take Ham home but once more after the night in Kentucky and he wasn't okay with that, not feeling good about himself for a while when it happened and he knew what Willie meant when he called her too fast.

When it was time to breeze, Willie said you better get Brumfield, this colt likes those jocks with quiet hands, so Ham lined him up and laughed when the jock said the same thing Thornburg had the first time he jumped off Smuggler.

"When this horse runs, I'm on him."

"That's a deal," said Ham.

They ran Snuggler in an allowance race on opening day, going seven furlongs from the Gulfstream chute and the result was never in question as Brumfield eased the black colt back in the early going, then let him roll from the quarter pole home to win by a neck.

Pamela had at least thirty people in the winner's circle picture but the next morning she was at the barn and told Ham she wanted to change jockeys because she thought

Brumfield gave Snuggler too much to do and should have had him near the lead.

"But he won going away," said Ham.

"He would have won by more if Jeffrey Fell rode him," she said.

"How do you figure?" said Ham as he felt himself slip into an imbroglio and sensed it wouldn't end well.

"Jeffrey's agent said he'd love to ride him," she said, "and I told him he could next time."

And when Ham objected she told him he had one horse when she found him and he could have one horse again if he wanted.

Fell hustled Snuggler to the lead and opened up two lengths going into the Clubhouse Turn but when he passed the three quarter pole and turned into the backstretch the colt was already done and stopped like he hit a wall.

Pamela just got up and left the box without a word before the race was over and a couple of dozen people followed her out.

When the vet told him Snuggler had bled like a stuck pig and he'd need three months off at least Ham kicked an empty water bucket about ten yards.

"Wasn't meant to be," said Willie.

Tony the van driver came by the next morning and told Ham sit down buddy 'cause you're not going to like what I have to tell you. He said Pamela had sent the van and it was there at the loading ramp, waiting to take the horses to her new trainer up at Payson Park, closer to where she lived.

"She said to tell you to send her a bill. Sorry, pal."

And when all the other horses were gone, Ham and Willie sat in those worn-out easy chairs at the end of the shedrow and Willie said son, go give Snuggler a carrot, he might be lonely.

CHAPTER 13

1978 - 79

Ham looked at that silver pocket watch every day but it never made him think of his grandfather, who had become a cloudy memory of an old man in a wicker rocking chair on the front porch of a concrete-block house in Rutland.

The one it did make him think of was his father and the last contact they'd had being when the man put it in his hand.

Ham hadn't heard from nor had he tried to contact his father since the day before he ran away from his mother's home five years ago, when he called the last number he had for him, wanting to talk and try to make some sense of life. But his old man hadn't answered that day and after half-a-dozen more tries he had packed his duffel bag and headed for the bus stop in Manchester down by the village center, thinking well now I'm on my own.

When Willie once asked what his father did, Ham just said he was a cop, not that he'd been Chief of Police and when he changed the subject Willie didn't push the issue, he just let it go.

It came as a surprise to Ham when his father left, because up until then everything about their home-life seemed so normal and it was all of a sudden when he sat the kids down and told them that things had changed with him and Ham's mother and that he was going away to the Caribbean and live on a sailboat no less with Missus Howe from down in the village.

Ham didn't even know his old man could sail, but when he thought about it hard, he recalled that his dad grew up in Mallets Bay on Lake Champlain and that's where that came from.

But where Missus Howell came from wasn't that hard to figure out. Her husband came back from the war in Korea with his mind messed up, what folks in town called "shell-shocked" and he took his refuge in a bottle of Cutty Sark.

They had no kids and it seemed like Ham's dad was always having to go to their house and haul him in for knocking her around, giving the man a night to dry out in the Manchester jail at least two or three times a month.

And Ham had seen some strain around the house when his sisters started getting older, not daddy's little girls anymore but wanting to wear makeup and short skirts and hang out listening to rock and roll with their friends and riding in cars with the high school guys who wore their hair greased back like Elvis and tucked a pack of Lucky Strikes in the sleeve of their white t-shirts.

But Ham's mother embarrassed him regularly enough too, wearing those same short skirts and behaving like she was a big sister instead of a mom and maybe flirting a bit too much with some of the teachers at the high school.

So when he overheard a guy like Mister Cooper the basketball coach saying something again about his mom's backside, maybe it had already been percolating in Hamilton Greer's mind that the guy needed a good punch in the mouth, and boy would he have liked to have had his old man to talk to after that but Dad was nowhere to be found.

Willie only got a small check from Social Security every month, so Ham counted up his resources and figured he might be able to keep feeding the two of them and Snuggler if he sold the trailer and maybe he'd be able to hold on to the pickup.

They'd both have to live off that until they got a horse or two to run for some purse money. The Racing Secretary at Gulfstream wasn't one to kick a guy when he's down, so he let Ham and Willie stay there even though they only had one horse that couldn't even race and told them he'd give them another stall or two in case they could find some more horses.

So it was a pleasant surprise when Pamela paid her bill right away and they didn't have to sell the trailer but they had no doubt what to do when the money arrived, they had to claim a horse.

Ham parked himself at the entrance to the paddock for the next week and when an Ohio-bred filly named Little Sheba turned up for $5,000, he and Willie decided she was their best chance.

The filly finished in the middle of the pack the day they took her, beaten a few lengths as she made the lead in a mile race and backed up down the lane, but Willie said not to worry, she was bred to be a sprinter and had no business in a route race anyway.

And when Ham ran into a trainer he knew from Jersey named Bubbles that told him he'd part with his maiden Good Day Sunshine for two thousand if it were to be a cash deal, they bought him too and put the bay gelding in the stall on the other side of the barn.

"Sunshine" was a five year old and even though he was still a maiden, he was another that had a habit of running in the money and Willie said he was probably never going to win except if he did it by accident.

Willie said horses run for one of two reasons; either they're running away, like their ancestors did to escape lions and bears, or they're chasing the pack in front of them, like kids do in follow-the-leader. He said Sunshine was one that was content to follow whoever was the leader and probably wouldn't know what to do when he got to the front by himself.

The old bay had been racing since he was two and had a dozen second-place finishes, which was actually okay for their situation, as Willie pointed out:

"You get the same money for three seconds as you do for a win even if you don't get your picture taken and when it comes right down to it, cash is cash and it all spends however you get it."

Ham and Willie had to hit the road when Gulfstream closed and they found themselves at Beulah Park for two reasons; primary was the fact that Little Sheba was a good deal faster than a lot of the other Ohio-bred fillies in that neck of the woods.

The other reason was that Beulah was a track that would give them stalls for those horses that wouldn't fit in at the higher tier tracks like Keeneland or Churchill or Monmouth or even Penn National and ringing in Ham's ears was Willie's admonition to stick to a small pond.

The Racing Secretary gave Ham three stalls in the round barn, and the neighbor to his left was a pig-farmer who liked to train his horses at home, jogging them around the perimeter of hog-filled wallows until they were fit, then shipping into Beulah for a few breezes before he entered in a race. Occupying the stalls to the right was an old cowboy with six Idaho-breds he legged up there before heading home to the gem state to race them at LeBois Park.

When Ham started to grouse about their humble surroundings, comparing them to the splendor of Saratoga and Hialeah, Willie waxed philosophical:

"Sometimes when you're not doing any good, best thing you can do is to take a step back and gather yourself up, see if the Good Lord finds you among those humble; those meek that He's going to let inherit the earth. 'Cause maybe He's the one what cut you down to size in the first place, when you got too big for your britches."

Even though he couldn't see, Willie made Ham set up a TV at the barn so he could listen along while Ham told him what was happening in the Triple Crown races.

The second time Alydar couldn't get past Affirmed Willie said you watch when they go to stud, maybe he beats him there, but he ain't never gonna beat him on that racetrack, this is another one of those years when a great one came along, maybe two great ones and a shame for that Mister Veitch, training the one was second best.

"It's a good thing he didn't have any hair to start with, 'cause that Affirmed would have made him pull it all out anyway," said Willie and he laughed hard at his own joke.

That summer was warmer than normal in Ohio and rainier than normal too. It seemed the track was always sloppy and Willie quipped that one thing that didn't matter to him anymore was if the sun was out, since he couldn't see it anyway, but he sure did appreciate that it wasn't cold since his old bones were starting to creak and everything hurt when he got up in the morning.

They took Little Sheba out to have a breeze one morning and had to do it on a muddy track and she skipped through the slop like a kid playing at the beach. She won the first time they ran her and it was a good thing she did or Ham might not have had enough money to pay their feed bill or the vet when they needed to ship the horses out to their next stop which was River Downs in Cincinnati.

And Willie said if the big black horse would get ready quick enough they could run him in a stakes race at that little track and there wouldn't be a horse in that neck of the woods that could even warm him up.

Willie was holding Snuggler's shank as the big colt nuzzled him.

"Looks good," said Ham.

"Looks good to me too," said Willie, laughing.

"I think he likes you," said Ham.

"What he likes is the peppermints in my shirt pocket," said Willie.

Willie said he'd talked to Garth Patterson and the jock said he'd be glad to come by and get on Snuggler anytime, not just for breezes like most jocks but he'd even gallop him if they wanted and Ham said thanks, we'll take all the help we can get.

Patterson had a Gulfstream trailer he pulled around the country and it was parked at the trailer park across the street from the stable gate and he had Ham and Willie over for supper one night. The jock was from Idaho and he travelled with a big white cockatoo named Kelso and he claimed he'd taught the bird to talk but when he tried to show off for them he couldn't get it to say a word.

They were sitting by the trailer watching the sun go down when the bird whistled at Patterson and he took it out of its cage and let it ride on his shoulder while they finished their apple pie and beer.

Ham said that's one smart bird and the jock said watch this and Kelso stood on one leg and raised his wing and his other leg and made a sound like he farted and Ham laughed so hard he fell out of the lawn chair.

River Downs reminded Ham of Saratoga, only smaller, and when a toad-strangler of a thunder storm came through one morning it made a lake between the barns that took him back to Mister Evans' barn and the first day he set foot on a race track. When he related the reminiscence to

Willie they both went silent for a spell, going back to the summer day when they met.

"You been through a lot of life in a little time," said Willie.

"Seems like a hundred years," said Ham.

They stood outside the racing office for a while, and one would say a name from the past like Spider or Lizzie or Toady and the other would start a story and they'd take turns finishing it.

Willie never mentioned Carla, thinking maybe that might still be a sore point with Ham and not wanting to hurt his feelings but Ham brought her up himself.

"I wrote to her a few times, sent her some poems," he said, "and she wrote me back once. 'Said she met a guy from L.A. who surfed and thought she was going to stay there but then she never answered any of the other ones I sent after that so I gave it up."

Ham found a little Italian place for them to eat, not far from the track and that was another reminder, taking them back to the red-checkered tablecloths down the street from Belmont.

"What are you, blind?" said the waitress.

"Huh?" said Willie.

She stared at him for a few moments and told him he looked like Ray Charles with those dark glasses on at night.

Willie bobbed his head and crooned *"Georgia, Georgia..."*

"Who had the ranch?" said the waitress, rolling her eyes and holding out a salad.

They'd go there once a week for the spaghetti and meatballs and every time they had the garlic bread Willie teased Ham and said to make sure he brushed his teeth before he tried to charm any pretty girls or they'd run away before he got a chance to kiss them.

When Snuggler finally got fit enough to run, the only spot he was eligible for was a little stakes race at a mile and a sixteenth but it turned out that Patterson had to be out of town that day, so they used a local kid named Garcia.

Garcia was an okay rider but not half the jockey Patterson was and when Snuggler got a little rank going to the first turn the jock pulled too hard on his mouth and the big colt fought back and bolted to the outside. They lost so much ground that when he finally got straightened out to make his run it was a case of too little too late and Snuggler barely got up for fourth money even though he'd been much the best.

Ham was fuming when the rider got back and as the kid told him Snuggler needed a pair of blinkers and a run-out bit, like it was the horse's fault, Willie held tight to his arm and said easy boy, don't make a bad deal worse, 'remember you got a different perspective that him.

Back at the barn Willie was walking Snuggler to cool him out and he called out to Ham to come have a look.

"He ain't right," said Willie, and when Ham felt the colt's knees and ankles they were okay but one of his feet was hot as a firecracker. The vet came and took an x-ray and sure enough, he'd cracked the coffin bone in his foot.

"No foot, no horse," said the vet, echoing the words Willie had told Ham a hundred times and they both knew the big black horse was done. The vet said Snuggler might make a riding horse for someone after a long vacation, but he was finished at the races.

So it was quite a shock when they ran Good Day Sunshine the first time at River Downs and he won and a kid from Chicago claimed him.

The six thousand dollars Ham got for him between the claim and the purse wasn't enough to go far, but all the bills were paid and Little Sheba was the only one left to feed after Ham gave Smuggler away to a lady who rehabilitated broken-down racehorses and turned them into riding horses for kids.

Since money was so tight they hadn't made a bet in ages, but after Little Sheba finished off the board in an Ohio-bred allowance race, Ham told Willie the saddle had slipped and it wasn't her fault and Willie said well here's our chance.

Two weeks later they put her in the trailer and hauled her up to Arlington Park in Chicago and she went off at eleven-to-one in a claiming race and the two thousand dollars they took a chance with turned into almost twenty. Ham told Willie we've had enough of this, we're going back to Tampa and we may end up broke, but at least we'll be warm and broke.

The last time he'd been at Tampa Bay Downs, Ham had made sure to make a proper exit, leaving a nice bottle of Kentucky bourbon with Crockett the stall man and the old guy didn't forget that.

He put them in three stalls in the last barn at the far end of the stable area where the afternoon breeze always moved the humid air around and the Little Sheba didn't get too bothered by the flies and the mosquitoes and he told Ham not to worry about filling those other stalls, you'll find something to claim when the rest of those bad trainers get here.

Ham stood by the paddock each day and made notes on the horses that passed by and he and Willie talked it over at supper.

"Maybe 'ought to think about taking that Riverman colt that 'been running sprints up north," said Willie, "Nothing like finding a horse that's bred to run on the grass and hasn't never set foot on it yet."

They claimed Old Suwannee for eight thousand and he finished last going six furlongs on the Tampa dirt track. When they got him back to the barn, Willie knelt and felt the gelding's feet.

"Round as a dinner plate, flat as a pancake," he said, "We never run him again anyplace but on the grass."

Ham was ready to raise Old Suwannee up the twenty-five percent and run him back in a claimer when Willie said didn't I teach you better, boy, put that horse in a starter handicap. There was a race coming up at a mile and an eighth, which was much further than Suwannee had ever gone, but when he drew an inside post and had the lowest weight to carry, Willie said now we should bet a little money.

Old Suwannee hadn't been doing anything but sprinting all his life, getting pushed hard and rushed to the front, so it was easy for the jockey to grab an early lead going into the Clubhouse Turn.

In fact, Manganello slowed the pace so much that the old gelding thought he was just out for a gallop and when the announcer said they passed the half-mile pole in fifty-one seconds, Willie said:

"Trottin' horse time, he won't get beat from there."

Ham stepped aside just as the track photographer took the win picture so it looked like Willie was the only one there, holding on to the horses' shank, and of course Willie didn't know until after when someone asked him how he could do that, train horses blind, and he just told them he didn't train the horses, he just talked to them.

And that wasn't far from the truth since most of the time while Willie walked the horses he was having a conversation with them, telling them stories of the great ones he'd seen like Man o'War and Citation and Secretariat and Ham swore those horses listened to the old man.

Ham told Willie he thought it might be a good time for them to go back to Kentucky, mainly because he thought Willie was getting a bit frail and might like to be closer to his home, but he didn't say that.

And Willie said that was a good idea, he'd like to smell the bluegrass again.

By springtime they were almost ready to head back north when Ham claimed another horse. He didn't talk it over as much as he usually did with Willie, just did it on the fly, an impulsive move made on the spur of the moment and when he got the mare back to the barn Willie walked the horse to cool her out and when he was done he shook his head.

"'This horse got a wild eye?" said Willie and Ham said yes but how would you know that and Willie said he could feel that nervousness right through the shank and I hope you can get out on this one before she loses her mind.

Ham waited an extra week and a half to leave Tampa just so he could have the thirty days pass to allow him to run the mare back there and drop her below the price he'd taken her for.

She went off the favorite and it was all she could do to beat a straggler and Ham breathed a sigh of relief when one of the local guys claimed her and when they got back to the barn Willie didn't say a thing about the horse, just can we leave now.

Latonia wasn't as charming as some of the old tracks they'd stabled at, but everything in the stable area had been recently renovated and Little Sheba and Old Suwannee were side-by-side on the sunny side of a nice barn near the quarter pole gap. Ham found nothing but disappointment when he went looking for the plaque on the Clubhouse wall with the names of the leading trainers that Mister Evans had told him about and Willie said they must have torn the wall down and forgot to put the plaque up when they rebuilt the place.

One morning Willie didn't get out of bed and told Ham he wasn't feeling that well and not up to walking any more horses and maybe could he take him home so he could have a visit with his sister, the last one of the family still there at the old house and when Ham dropped him off on that Friday, Willie had a tough time getting up the steps.

Ham got back to the house on Sunday night and Willie's sister was sitting there on the front steps, clutching the handkerchief she used to wipe her eyes.

"He's gone," she said.

"Gone where?" said Ham.

"Gone to the Lord," she said, "up there with the angels on high."

Hamilton Greer was twenty-two years old and feeling very much alone in the world when he sat on a cot in the tack room at Latonia and held the transistor radio he and Willie had listened to for the past six years.

Ham held it like it was a baby, cradled in his arms, and imagined he could hear Willie's voice, speaking in that soft way he used to coach a young boy from childhood to manhood and he cried himself to sleep on Willie's cot.

CHAPTER 14

1978-79

Hamilton Greer lost his way for a while after Willie passed and his life became a desultory wandering as he avoided even the slightest engagement with his fellow man and became a near recluse, hair to his shoulders and a stranger to his shaving razor.

He remained at Latonia for another month and a half and took his horses to the track each morning to train but he never ran Little Sheba or Old Suwannee the whole time and finally he sold each of them and his trailer too. The money he received for the lot was enough to settle his debts but little more.

He got a couple of hundred from the tack man for his exercise saddle and bridles and a trainer on the other side of the barn bought his wall plaques and cross ties and webbings and he kept the leather shank with the brass plate with his name on it that Willie had given him one year for his birthday. The rest of his gear fit neatly in the back of the pickup and when he stopped at the gas station to fill up, he asked the attendant for an Eastern U.S. roadmap.

"Where 'you headed?" said the man.

"All roads lead to home," said Ham.

"I thought that was Rome," said the man.

"I guess you never know," said Ham.

Ham drove to Willie's family cemetery where they'd put him in the ground beside his mama and papa and grandma and grandpa and he sat there on the ground for a while and talked to his old friend's headstone before he lay down in the bluegrass next to it and fell into a deep sleep.

And he dreamed that they were in the stands at Hialeah as Flamingos circled the infield lake and when he asked his questions about why things happened the way they did Willie said you'll find out soon enough boy and the sun was setting when he finally awoke and said good-bye.

Ham kept the transistor radio on the front seat of the pickup and once in a while he'd run his hand across the top of it and when he stopped for the night at a little motel by the Cumberland Gap he brought the radio in the room where he drank a few beers and listened to music until he fell off into an uneasy sleep.

In his dream he was walking in the middle of a racetrack with Willie and a dozen horses were passing them, not in a race, but rider-less in a pack like wild mustangs. And he and Willie laughed at nothing until inside the racetrack rail they could see J.B. lashing a horse with a bullwhip and when he moved toward him Ham walked right out of the dream and it took him a while to get back to sleep.

The next morning Ham awoke a little foggy and he drove for an hour or so before he realized he'd been heading south while he meant to go east, so when he stopped to get gas he pulled out his road map and plotted a new way up through the Blue Ridge Mountains to get back on course.

At one point he thought he saw the same hillside that he thought he had seen from the window of the horse van in Tennessee but of course he'd never been there before and in some ways all mountainsides look the same.

Outside of Hagerstown, Maryland, he stopped at a roadside stand and got a burger and some fries and parked by the side of a brook that ran through smooth round rocks and made a chirping sound and he washed down his lunch with a bottle of beer in a brown paper bag while he studied the map.

He drove another hour and pulled into a rest area and it was a warm evening so he propped himself up with his duffel bag in the truck bed and read a biography of Thomas Jefferson and he fell asleep right there as he tried to figure out how someone who signed a paper that said all men were created equal could own slaves.

Ham had halfway thought about trying to make it back to Saratoga by his birthday but by the time he got through Maryland he was tired of being alone and on the road, so he drove through the stable gate at Delaware Park and parked his truck by the track kitchen while he went to get lunch and consider his options.

Before he finished his meatloaf with mushroom gravy and mashed potatoes a groom he knew from Tampa asked him if he was looking for a job and he said yeah what the hell, here's as good a place as any for right now. He went to the grandstand and got a haircut and a shave and looked himself in the mirror and said that's enough Greer, time to move on with your life.

It had been over a year since Willie had told him that Spectacular Bid might just be the next Triple Crown winner except it's tough enough to win with a good jockey, let alone some kid that doesn't have any experience, and when the grey horse lost the Belmont Ham figured Willie was right, it wasn't a safety pin that stopped him, but using a rider who wasn't up to the task.

"Like having some rookie 'pitch to Reggie Jackson, 'he's going to get et' for lunch," Willie had said, "He might be okay in the minor league but up in top-class, it's taking a knife to a gunfight."

Ham thought about those conversations while he watched from the rail at the Delaware paddock as Buddy Delp gave his rider a leg up on Spectacular Bid.

He knew Willie would have said that big grey colt won by as far as you can throw a rock and next day he read the writer's comment in the *Morning Telegraph* that Shoemaker barely moved his hands when he won by seventeen lengths and Ham thought he would have told Willie that he could have ridden that horse himself and it still would have won.

Ham considered himself lucky at least that he didn't have to share a tack room with anyone. The trainer he went to work for was a short, chubby man that everyone called Jelly because those were his favorite donuts and it seemed like he always had one in his hand.

Jelly was one of those guys who you could always tell what he had for breakfast by the remnants on his shirt, but he was a good horseman and after a few days, he and Ham each knew the other knew their way around a horse.

They compared notes:

"Saratoga?" said Ham.

"Never been there," said Jelly.

"Belmont?"

"Nope."

"Hialeah?"

"Couldn't even spell it," said Jelly, "But I ran one at Charles Town in the West Virginia Derby a couple 'years ago. Got ten grand for finishing fourth with a home-bred."

The Jelly Stable consisted of a dozen horses and Jelly owned them all and had bred most of them and between he and his son Junior and Ham, they rubbed twelve of the best turned out hides that ran at Delaware Park that summer.

Jelly paid well and always in cash and the four maidens that Ham took care of had ordinary pedigrees, but he treated them all as if they were special and the first two he ran were in cheap maiden races but they won like they were stakes horses.

Ham never saw Jelly go the betting windows until the day they ran one of the two year olds for the first time and as the horses left the paddock he said to Ham follow me.

Jelly was out of breath and panting like a dog by the time they finished climbing the back stairs to the second floor and he led Ham through one door into the men's room and out another and when he was sure no one was following them they went to a ten dollar window and he told Ham bet whatever you have in your pocket kid, this one won't get beat.

The next week when the winners circle pictures came, Jelly gave one to Ham and made a joke about how the three of them, him and Ham and Junior, how they all looked like cats that just had a big canary lunch.

Delaware Park racetrack sat in a hollow and on those days in the middle of summer when the air got still and damp, it could feel as stifling as a tropical rain forest in the Amazon. Most of the trainers set up huge box fans at each end of their shedrows just to move the air around and blow the mosquitoes away so their poor sweating horses could have some relief.

And there weren't but a few air conditioners in the stable area, so for most folks it was too hot to go to sleep early and every Sunday night lots of the racetrackers living on the backstretch would gravitate to a boxing ring behind the rec hall where anyone was free to step up and put on gloves.

The pugilists strutted when they got in the ring, calling themselves Rocky, Sugar Ray, Willie Pep and having those famous names embroidered on the back of their robes and once the bell rang they bobbed and weaved as if they were at Madison Square Garden.

The boxers had to wear headgear so no one would take too bad a beating and the announcer made a disclaimer that it was just for entertainment purposes, but you could tell the guys who showed up to fight had visions of Muhammad Ali and Leon Spinks inspiring them.

Junior was made just like his old man, short and stocky, but he was light enough on his feet and still small enough to get in the ring with the jockeys and exercise boys.

Jelly and Ham acted as corner men for Junior and Ham thought it was a joke until the fight started.

As the bell rang the exercise boy everybody called Cowboy did a quick little Ali-shuffle and popped Junior on the chin and he went down like a sack of Idaho potatoes and Ham held his breath for a moment while he waited for Junior to move.

Cowboy was strutting about the ring, arms raised to exhort the crowd over his knockout punch as he went to his corner and he figured the fight was all over until the ref told him it wasn't. He was so surprised to see Junior on his feet that he put his hands out to touch gloves and didn't think to raise them in time to deflect the roundhouse that laid him out.

After Willie's funeral a woman had introduced herself to Ham and said she was Willie's daughter Mariah and she handed him a shoebox, held shut with twine from a straw-bale.

"Daddy asked me to give you this, and he told me to tell you that you should open it on your next birthday but not before then."

Mariah said her father had told her he loved Ham like a son and she was very happy to meet him and see what a fine young man he was and she said she was grateful for that.

Ham did as he was told and waited until his birthday to open the box and when he did he was alone in a tack room at Delaware Park.

The shoebox was filled with old track programs and photos of some of the great horses Willie had been around, and on top of the pile was the one of him and Willie with Delilah in the winner's circle at Saratoga.

Taped to the inside of the box was a sheet of white paper, neatly folded and addressed in Willie's hand with the words "Ham and Eggs" and he opened it and read:

Dear Hamilton Greer,

Thank you for making the last few of an old man's years some of the best. You are as good a person as any I ever met. Always remember that the past will guide you as you look forward to your future. And never be afraid to take a chance.

Your friend Willie

In the bottom of the box was a yellowed diploma from the Kentucky State Industrial College that was inscribed with Willie's name and below his name it read Magna Cum Laude for studies in American History.

Jelly and Junior never raced during the winter, they just shipped their horses home to the farm in West Virginia and rested them until spring.

"You can use 'em up or save 'em up," said Jelly, and he liked to save 'em. Most of his horses were seven or eight years old and hadn't run more than half-a-dozen times a season since they started racing. Missus Jelly stayed at their farm all year round in a little house on fifty acres with a nice big barn and she only showed up at the racetrack if one of the babies she'd foaled was making its first start and she never called them by their real name, just the pet-name she'd given them.

When one would win their debut, Jelly would have the track photographer put that pet name on the picture and she had a whole wall full of Snookies and Shortys and Muscles and Cupcakes in her kitchen.

Jelly said his wife liked animals better than people and that's why she preferred to stay close to home with the chickens and ducks and pigs and the bunch of old retired horses that all thought they'd died and gone to horse-heaven.

When Jelly told Ham he was welcome to come home with them and watch the sun set on the Blue Ridge Mountains, but the winter days would be as short as the pay, Ham declined the offer and said no thanks sir but I'll see you down the road.

Ham wanted to get up to Stowe and see everyone before winter set in and he stayed at the house his mother and Steve bought when they finally sold the place in Manchester. The house was an old mustard yellow Victorian with two tall peaks and scalloped shingles under the eaves of its mansard roof and it was surrounded by a maple grove like the one where Ham had worked when he was a kid in the spring when everyone tapped the trees and drew out the sap into galvanized buckets to make maple syrup.

Steve had turned the garage into a wood shop and he invited Ham out there to sit in one of the easy chairs and have a beer while he sanded rungs for the new banister he was making for his wife as an anniversary present. They didn't talk much, just about the weather and how fast the leaves had turned this year and when Steve went quiet, Ham did too and let him work through an uncomfortable silence.

Ham's mom made him pancakes for the three days he spent with them and on those mornings he slept in for the first time in years and on the fourth day he packed up his gear, kissed each of his sisters and step-sisters and his Mom on the cheek and shook Steve's hand before he aimed the pickup truck toward the Florida panhandle and took the wild, winding ride down Route 100.

When he passed through Londonderry, Ham decided to cut over to Manchester and maybe stop there for lunch but as he drove through the town center and saw the park where he'd played as a kid he felt a touch of melancholy so he kept right on going down Route 7.

He had another pang when he passed Green Mountain Park in Pownal and realized that the Thoroughbreds were gone and it had been turned into a dog track and out of curiosity he drove through the parking lot that skirted the old stable area and saw a guy walking two greyhounds.

"What happened to the horses?" said Ham.

"After a while nobody came," said the dog walker, "Sad..."

Ham stayed on the scenic route through Massachusetts until he made his way west onto the Taconic Parkway and reflected that although he had nothing against dogs, but that did seem a sorry fate for such a nice little track.

The old Albany Post Road along the Hudson River passed through Ossining and when he saw a couple of billboards announcing that it was the home of Sing Sing prison, it occurred to Ham that that was where Spider was, like they said, "up the river," doing his time and maybe he'd better stop and see how the little guy was holding up.

He followed a couple of road signs and found himself in the parking lot, looked up at the massive prison walls and considered for a moment what a foreboding place it was.

Even though his dad had been the Chief of Police, Manchester was a small town, and the jail house there only had two cells and as far as Ham could remember the most desperate criminal they'd ever housed was Reverend Dawes, the minister who got drunk one night and set the Presbyterian church house on fire.

Ham accidentally left his driver's license in the truck but he had his track license among the few dollars in his pocket and the guards got a laugh out of that since they all knew Spider was a jockey.

"Here for the Sing Sing Derby?" said one.

And it was slightly unnerving to Ham as a guard frisked him and when the hefty iron door slammed behind him, it made a dull echo in the windowless room.

Ham sat across from a furtive, gaunt Spider and they spoke through a glass window with wire mesh and he couldn't help but ask the inane.

"Are you okay?" he said and wished he didn't.

"Thirteen months, three weeks and two days," said Spider, "Counting days for good behavior."

He told Ham it was a brutal place and if he weren't in for working for the mobsters and having some protection from them, he'd have hung himself by now. And how he felt so isolated there and that Ham was the first person he'd had visit and that hurt but his father was in Chester, Pennsylvania and that sounded like a worse place. They weren't even allowed to talk on the phone.

Spider said they still had the electric chair there that they called "Old Sparky," the one they'd fried the Rosenbergs in, but they didn't use it any more.

Ham asked him what he'd do when he got out and Spider just turned somber and shook his head.

"Only was one thing I ever wanted to do, but that's done."

Ham drove for the next few hours lost in thoughts of that conversation with Spider and wondered if maybe he shouldn't quit the racetrack and look for a life somewhere else, where folks didn't live such a fast life.

CHAPTER 15

1979-80

It was another meandering journey that Hamilton Greer found himself on that fall, forsaking the interstate system to instead travel the local highways and byways. He wanted to see those little towns and villages up close, the ones whose names he'd only seen on expressway exit signs as they rolled by on the horse vans.

The truth was, Ham didn't really have a plan, just took to the road and followed his nose to see where it might take him. If you could say there was any plan at all it was to get to familiar ground in Florida and he reckoned he had enough money to survive for a while when he got there, as not to be forced into taking a job he didn't want with people he didn't know. He knew he'd been lucky to find Jelly and that probably wouldn't happen again.

Ham passed through Middleburg and considered stopping in at the training center for a visit but decided he didn't want to bring back bittersweet memories of the time that he and Snuggler spent there so he just kept driving.

He hardly thought about horses at all until he stopped at a diner in Purcellville for some lunch and the waitress asked him what he liked for next spring's Derby.

"Plugged Nickle will be favorite, I guess," he said, "But he looks like a sprinter to me."

She took a confidential tone and spoke behind the back of her hand as if she were revealing a deep secret.

"The Firestone people down the road have that good filly with Mister Jolley, 'n a lot of folks hereabouts think she might beat the boys," she said.

"Hard for a filly to beat the boys," said Ham.

Fall was hanging on to an Indian Summer and it was worth a break now and then to enjoy the countryside, so he tried to vary his pace, sometimes travelling only a few hundred miles in a day and taking the time to pull over and investigate whenever he saw a historical marker.

In Albemarle County Ham made a detour to visit Monticello and he bought another book about Jefferson and the other Fathers of the American Revolution, and every so often he'd pull the pickup into a rest area and fall asleep on the grass, dozing off as he read about the same history that Willie liked to recall for him.

After he traversed North Carolina in only a few hours he decided to divert a bit at the South Carolina border so he could pass through Camden and Aiken to have a look at the place that Mister Evans had talked about so much and sure enough for miles and miles there was nothing but four-board fences surrounding thoroughbred racehorses.

A weathered grandpa at a roadside stand was selling fresh peanuts cooked in peanut oil and they were still warm and the slightest bit spicy, just the way Ham liked them, and he stayed for a while and talked as they sat at a wooden table and drank sweet iced tea poured into paper cups from a metal pitcher.

The old man told him it was a nice place to live around there, not too many people and of the ones that were, nobody was in too much of a hurry, and please y'all come back and see us again now.

Ham decided to stop outside Aiken to spend the night and he was at a service station topping off his gas tank so he wouldn't have to do it in the morning when he saw a boy of maybe eight or nine riding bareback on a flea-bitten grey.

The kid rode right up to Ham's pickup and asked him if he could please turn on the hose and give his horse a drink and Ham did that and the boy said thank you kindly sir before he rode away.

The following morning Ham was barely under way when he came upon a foreign car pulled to the roadside with a flat and there was a well-dressed woman staring at the offending tire with her hands on her hips and she gave it a good kick.

"Need some help with that?" said Ham.

"Just if you can fix this Goddamn tire," she said, and after Ham put on the spare she tried to give him two dollars and when he said no thank you Ma'am it's my pleasure she said what do I look like an old lady, don't call me Ma'am, it's Missus Glass.

"Where do you work?" she said.

"Just passing through," said Ham.

"Looking for work?" she said and Ham thought for a beat before he said maybe.

"Follow me," she said.

They pulled into the parking lot of a brand new Seven-Eleven store and Ham followed her around the building, the back of which hadn't even been painted yet. She asked him where he was from and where he'd been and what he'd done and told him she and her husband owned the grocery in town but they were branching out and if he wanted to it was easy work, to make sure the shelves were stocked and watch that nobody steals anything.

Inside there were two boys, barely teenagers, unpacking boxes and they snapped to attention when the woman walked in and barked at them.

"What have you been doing?" she said to the taller kid.

"He ate two ice cream sandwiches," said the kid, using an offense as his best defense.

"This is Mister Greer and he's going to be running the place. Do what he tells you," she said and turned on her heel.

Ham hustled to follow her out the front door.

"Excuse me?" he said, "Running the place?"

"You need a job and I need somebody to look after it. A hundred and twenty a week and you can stay over there for nothing, we own that too," she said, pointing at the motor court across the street.

"Go see Charlotte, she'll give you a cabin," she said and held out a fold of cash.

He looked at the money and he looked at the cabins and then he looked at the lady.

"Okay," he said.

"I'll show you everything you need to know tomorrow," and as she turned to go he said:

"Yes Ma'am."

And that made her spin around.

"Beverley. Beverley or Missus Glass, but not Ma'am," she said and left without another word.

Ham was there a month, getting Missus Glass' Seven-Eleven running just like his shedrow at the racetrack, opening and closing on time, merchandise on the shelves all straight and the windows shining. He planted some flowers in a couple of old wooden barrels and put them outside the front doors and told Beverly don't bother to pave the parking lot, it's better to hear the tires crunch the gravel so you know when someone's coming.

Ham hired a couple named Johnson that lived down the road to help him and it worked out fine for all since they had a bunch of kids and needed part time work and Ham was thereabouts all the time but needed someone to spell him occasionally.

He rarely left the place except for a couple of Saturdays when he wandered over to the grounds where they held the steeplechase races. Those fascinated Ham, especially when the riders passed by on the way to the paddock and he could see that most of them were almost as big as him, not like the diminutive jockeys who rode on the flat.

Ham and the Johnsons had just finished filling the coolers with soda and beer and sat down on the bench outside the front door to take a break when a horse van pulled in the parking lot.

The driver looked familiar coming across the parking lot and sure enough it was Tony, dropping off some horses and picking up some others to go on to Florida.

"Last place on earth I'd expect to see you," said Tony, "What the hell are you doing here?"

"I guess I needed a break," said Ham.

"Sorry to hear about your man Willie, he was a good one."

"The best," said Ham.

About two or three times a week the kid with the flea-bitten grey would come by and Ham would water his horse while the kid went to the men's room.

One afternoon Beverly pulled up just as the kid was leaving and her face went hard when she asked Ham who was that.

"That's Devon, he's the first one I met when I came here, 'watered his horse at the Sunoco station. He stops by on the way home from school a couple 'times a week."

"Tell him the bathroom's out of order," said Beverly, "and make sure the coloreds' drink from the hose, not the fountain, that's the rules."

Ham studied her unkind countenance for what seemed a long spell before he handed her his set of keys.

"Those are not the rules I follow," he said and he walked across the street and packed up.

Ham read the sign that said "Georgia 3 Miles" just before he glanced in his rearview mirror and saw the red lights flashing on top of the patrol car.

"Vermont?" said the cop.

"Yessir," said Ham.

"You're under arrest," said the cop and he put handcuffs on Ham while another officer poked through Ham's possessions.

The courthouse was a room on the back of an old white house with tall columns flanking the front door. The officer urged Ham to the counter and a silver haired man in a black robe told him he'd been accused of stealing from the new Seven-Eleven and it wasn't much use for Ham to deny it, just his word against Missus Glass and her husband the state senator.

Ham spent the night in one of the two cells in the back of the jailhouse but he got no sleep at all with the drunken man in the other cell throwing up and snoring like a chain saw until he did finally pass out.

Just after ten in the morning the Sheriff unlocked the cell and told Ham he was free to go, that Missus Glass said there must have been a mistake, probably some school kid had taken the charcoal and she said to tell Ham if he had followed the rules it wouldn't have happened.

It was midnight when Ham pulled up to the stable gate at Tampa Bay Downs, hoping that Treyvon would be working and lucky enough, he was.

"Who you with, Ham?" said Trey.

"Starting fresh," said Ham and he asked if there were an empty tack room he might stay in for the night and he'd look for a job in the morning.

"Five-B," said Trey, handing him a key. "That new lady trainer is looking for help. She doesn't get in too early."

"What's her name?" said Ham.

"Collins, Lizzie Collins," said Trey.

Ham sat on a straight chair at the end of the shedrow outside the office door at about six am and watched a couple of Mexican grooms that paid him no mind as they got their horses ready.

He was still there waiting when Lizzie's little Mercedes pulled up at quarter past seven. She didn't see him and sat in her car for a few minutes waiting for a song on the radio to finish.

"I heard you were looking for an exercise boy," said Ham.

"Yeah, perfect, a six-foot-two exercise boy to ride the camel," said Lizzie, "What are you up to, handsome?"

"Trey said you were training."

"If you could call it that. I'd likely not have a job if I wasn't sleeping with the boss," said Lizzie. "What I need is a good assistant to do all the work while I do interviews and cocktail parties."

"Then I guess I'm your man," said Ham and then she asked where's your partner and he told her about Willie passing and they both had a good cry right there in the shedrow.

By the time Lizzie's husband came out on Saturday morning Ham had some palms planted and flowers hung in the eaves and the shedrow was raked flat with the new white sand he'd gotten maintenance to deliver.

Judge Collins might have been twice Lizzie's age but he was handsome and trim and fit and only a few inches shorter than her and he followed her around like a puppy dog. When he exulted over the barn's appearance, Lizzie winked at Ham and told him give me the bills and I'll pay them in cash.

Lizzie had a barn full of horses she'd acquired, mostly from sales and a couple privately, but she said her husband wouldn't let her claim, his opinion being that wasn't the way classy people got a good one.

Ham and Lizzie went through the whole barn and he took notes: three sound colts, three sound fillies and a dozen and a half limpers.

"We can't run them for a tag," said Lizzie.

"We can't win if we don't," said Ham. "And trust me, the Judge will eventually get sick of nothing but bills and no winners."

A few days later Lizzie managed to get to the barn at daybreak and Ham had the whole stable ready for a workout. He handed her a stopwatch and a chart on a clipboard with each horses' name written on it.

"Miguel will bring them out two at a time," he said and they sat in a box at the finish line while all twelve breezed from the three-eighths pole to the wire and galloped out.

"Looks like a good bit of chaff and not a lot of wheat," said Lizzie when they were done.

"Two colts, two fillies," said Ham, "and the rest will have to go."

The fillies had each won in maiden special at big prices, but that was way back in August when Lizzie got her trainer's license at Monmouth and it had been a drought ever since.

So it took all of Lizzie's powers of persuasion but she managed to convince her husband that they take the little two year old colt named Rusty Nails that Judge Collins had paid fifty thousand for and put him in a thirty thousand maiden claimer and he won by a desperate nose but you'd have thought it was a stakes race the way he celebrated his wife's victory.

For the next month they ran the slow horses in bottom claimers and they all got taken and finished nowhere when they did and that pleased the Judge almost as much as the trips to the winners circle when the fast ones won.

Back when they worked for Bogie, Willie had told Ham about how lots of successful folks did it, not worrying about who got credit as long as the job got done and that's what he knew was the only thing that would work in Lizzie's barn.

He trained the horses and schooled the grooms and when they saddled up in the paddock he held the horses' heads while he let Lizzie tighten the girth as her husband beamed.

Ham could see that Judge Collins liked the horses... but he loved Lizzie...

By the middle of February they were down to eight horses and only one of the better horses was still looking for a win but the Judge had caught the racing bug full strength.

He let Lizzie place the horses in any kind of race she wanted, even if it meant their getting claimed and losing money, as long as they won their share and she was having fun.

The best colt in the barn was the three year old Black Robe and Ham worked him in near darkness a few times just as the track opened, and Franklin the clocker said he didn't catch him, he was too early.

"How'd he go?" said Franklin.

"Half in forty seven?" said Ham.

"Half in forty-eight and three?" said Franklin and Ham smiled, as they knew he'd shared a secret again.

Black Robe was twelve to one on the morning line in a tough maiden special on the last Saturday of the meet and Lizzie and the Judge brought a dozen friends to the paddock.

"What do you think?" said the Judge.

"Got a good chance," said Ham and the Judge turned to his entourage.

"Hamilton says we can't lose," said the Judge, and when he headed to the betting queues Ham watched as the odds on the tote board dropped until the colt was favorite.

And when Black Robe finished five lengths clear at the wire, the Judge turned to Ham and said, "Told you so..."

Lizzie came to the barn on the last week of April and announced to Ham that she and the Judge were going off to buy a farm in Kentucky and a house in Saratoga and wasn't life grand.

"Clifton says we should take a holiday after we go to Derby," said Lizzie, pronouncing it "Darby" and she handed Ham her checkbook with all the blank checks signed and the keys to her Mercedes and told him to look after things until they got back from their cruise in the Caribbean.

"We'll catch up with you at Monmouth," she said.

Spring was the quiet time around Tampa as the racing wound down and Ham found a little crab-shack with a view of the bay where he especially liked to go for the oysters they brought from the Gulf of Mexico up near the mouth of the Apalachicola River and he'd put the red sauce and horseradish on them and wash them down with a cold beer or two.

The shack had a huge color television over the bar so he made a point of getting there early on the first Saturday in May to find himself a good seat to watch the Kentucky Derby. There weren't any other racetrackers around but just about everyone in the place had an opinion on who'd win.

"I bet on Plugged Nickle, he looks like a cinch," said a college kid, "Who do you like?"

"Maybe the filly," said Ham and they watched as Plugged Nickle battled with the other favorite, Rockhill Native, until they knocked each other out and faded.

He thought back to the diner in Virginia where the waitress had told him Genuine Risk might be the first filly to beat the boys in seventy years and dang if she wasn't right.

"How'd you know?" said the kid.

"Always listen to waitresses," said Ham and he wasn't sure, but he thought he might have seen Lizzie and the Judge there on TV, crowded into the group having their picture taken with the chestnut filly.

CHAPTER 16

1980

By the end of June the weather at the New Jersey shore can be almost as hot and humid as Florida and Ham needed those enormous box-fans to move the air or the horses would almost melt in their stalls unless a thunderstorm came by to clear out the mugginess.

Ham was more than slightly uncomfortable with his situation as the Fourth of July weekend approached and Lizzie and the Judge had yet to show their faces at Monmouth. He was okay with running the barn day-to-day and making decisions about the horses' welfare and even about racing them when he thought they were ready but he wasn't okay at all with losing them at the claiming box or having the purse money pile up and the bills go unpaid.

The signed checks Lizzie left him with had sufficed to finish up business in Tampa and relocate to Monmouth, but the feed man and the tack man and the vet and the blacksmith... they all wanted to get paid on time.

So it was a huge relief for Ham that afternoon when a black Cadillac Sedan de Ville pulled up at the barn and Judge and Missus Collins disembarked, albeit two months to the day they'd left him alone in Tampa. And to listen to them, it was like they'd been gone overnight.

They told Ham to put on a clean shirt and they'd take him out to dinner and fill him in all the juicy details of what they'd been up to between their trips to Kentucky and Saratoga and Barbados, and when he asked if they wanted to see the horses, they said we can do it tomorrow.

Racetrackers have a tradition of seeking out the best Neopolitan food the same way gangsters do, and when they pulled into the portico at Frank's Continental in West End, the crowd lined up at the watering hole was a cliché of the mob joints in Little Italy, Brioni-suited men and platinum blondes wall-to-wall.

Ham had heard about the restaurant but he'd never had the cash to frequent a place where the menus didn't have prices on them and he felt somewhat out of place there in his chambray shirt and jeans.

The Judge took an embrace and a kiss on the cheek from the maitre'd and by the time they got to their table he'd stopped more times than a guy running for mayor.

"Guaranteed winner next week," said the Judge sotto voce to a couple of the guys in the expensive threads and one of them sent a bottle of wine to the table and after dinner a plate of cannolis arrived.

"What can we run that's sure to win?" said the Judge.

Ham was beginning to get warm and said maybe we can drop one of the maidens way down and excuse me please I need to go to the men's room.

He walked out the front door and into the parking lot to get some air but didn't linger there, uncomfortable around the drivers with their black suits and their shiny black sedans and when he got back there was one of the Judge's friends at the table sitting in his seat.

"Hamilton... Carmine... Carmine, this is Hamilton, he's my wife's assistant trainer," said the Judge and the man grasped Ham's hand with an iron grip before he exited with the rest of the finely manicured crew.

Folks around Monmouth were accustomed to dealing with Ham and lots thought he was the trainer when they'd come to the barn and they'd ask for "E.B. Collins" which was the way Lizzie put her name in the program.

He got used to her Mercedes showing up at the barn randomly and worked out the training charts himself and after the first month Lizzie was near the top of the trainer's list for wins.

Ham found a little bar in Monmouth Beach called Boyle's, just one room with a pool table and a dartboard where the locals drank the Guinness on tap and everyone imagined they were in Ireland. He'd slide over in the evening for a shot and a beer, eat his supper at the bar and make it a night before nine.

One evening he sat next to a Jamaican jockey named Felix who had dark skin and a fine thin aristocratic nose. Felix claimed to have been leading rider in the Caribbean but he wasn't getting any mounts at Monmouth, so if Ham needed someone he was the guy to call and by the way he was light and you won't find anyone who can work a horse as well.

Felix turned out to be a good hand and pretty soon he was galloping and breezing every horse in the barn and Ham put him on a couple of the cheaper ones and they ran well and Felix got himself an agent and began to ride for other trainers too.

A few of Lizzie's runners finished first even though Ham thought they weren't good enough and Ham just figured they got lucky but one afternoon when they won with one of those longshots the horse's tail switched from the quarter pole to the wire and a pair of State police grabbed Felix as he made the walk back to the jock's room.

The same Troopers came back to the barn and told Ham they caught Felix with a buzzer and asked what would he know about that.

"Surprise to me," said Ham, "but I thought those horses ran awful good for him."

"Where's the trainer?" said one of the Troopers, and Ham told him Lizzie was away, fixing up her new house at Saratoga and no he didn't think she bet on any of the horses, he'd never seen her put more than two bucks on anything.

The Trooper didn't bother to ask Ham if he did and after they left he sat alone in the tack room for a while before he could catch his breath.

The following week they ran the best maiden filly they had at Monmouth, the one Lizzie paid almost a hundred thousand for and Ham made sure he put the bandages on himself, hoping that anyone who checked would see the big bend in its tendon where he'd set the cotton to make it look like a bow. He knew the horse might win in maiden special, but the Judge wanted a winner and putting her in a high claimer made that as sure as he could.

He led the filly through the tunnel from the track to the paddock and he could see Lizzie and the Judge along with half a dozen guys that could have been extras in a Godfather film and when he looked up at the tote board their horse was even money.

And the race itself played out like a Hollywood script, as Phil Grimm rattled the reins when the gates opened and the filly quickly opened up a few lengths and he never looked back.

Ham bit his lip while he watched for a claim tag to appear in the winner's circle, but it never did, and as he went to follow the groom and his horse back to the test barn the Judge hailed him.

"Get me ten pictures for my friends, would you kid?" he said, and Ham said no problem, you're the boss.

When Genuine Risk finished second in the Belmont stakes she became the only filly ever to hit the board in all three of the Triple Crown races. Ham would like to have seen her in the flesh but there wasn't much chance she'd come to Monmouth and anyway he was busier than a Manhattan cab driver on Saturday night so he settled for watching the replay on the evening news.

But he was at the paddock like any other railbird when the fans packed Monmouth for their Invitational, the local version of a classic and he cashed a nice ticket when Thanks to Tony, a Jersey-bred colt stabled on the other side of his barn won going away to upset the heavy-heads from out of town.

And he was sorry they had to ship to Saratoga before Spectacular Bid's visit when the champ came to Monmouth and dusted Canada's best mare, Glorious Song, but at least he'd had his chance to see the champ at Delaware.

The Judge didn't do anything but go first-class, so when he and Lizzie arrived at Saratoga they kept a regular table at Siro's and they went out dancing nearly every night with a chic crowd of socialites and a bunch of hangers-on.

Lizzie's running mate Stella was sharp featured and long legged and she liked to wear her blonde hair in bangs like Lizzie's. Her husband was a prissy little guy named Reggie who sported a bow tie and told everyone he'd been a bloodstock agent but now he was retired and the Judge asked Lizzie if retired at the track meant you didn't have to pick up the check anymore and she said exactly.

Ham was finally feeling like himself again and it was only occasionally that he'd succumb to a wave of nostalgia, like when he would pass the farmers' market across from the park and stop to buy a hand melon the way he and Willie used to do. He would take it back to the barn and make a mid-afternoon snack when everyone was gone and he could enjoy the solitude and the company of Lizzie's horses.

He was happy enough with everything at the barn until the Judge decided to start entertaining and hired a chef to make breakfast every morning. They put up a little tent at the front of the barn that forced Ham to route the horses out the back in order to avoid the Bloody Mary drinkers eating omelets right in his usual path to the track.

"Sorry," was all Lizzie would say.

The Judge wanted her to ask the Racing Secretary why they couldn't have a barn up near the track but Lizzie told her husband that being in the last row of barns wasn't a slight, it was the best place to be since the horses didn't need to be near the action, they needed peace and quiet but Ham thought she should maybe practice what she preached.

Ham and Lizzie started to bicker some when folks wandered in the shedrow with cigarettes and drinks and when Ham saw one of Lizzie's girlfriends feeding hors d'ouvres to one of the horses he ordered the woman out of the barn.

"Lighten up," said Lizzie,

"It's Saratoga."

The Judge had smartened up enough to let Lizzie wear the pants when it came to racing, figuring out that he had been burned a few times trying to play the game, getting sold horses that couldn't outrun a possum and most of the time it seemed he was happy enough to play the doting husband.

Lizzie proved a good actor herself, and you'd have been hard pressed to figure that she was actually a Cockney from London's east end and didn't grow up amongst royalty herself.

"Clifton, darling, you spoil me so..." she said when he bought her another horse.

"They all look like big brown dogs to me," said the Judge.

The hot streak they had at Tampa and the winners at Monmouth were all in the past and the Judge had plenty in the new entourage who liked to remind him that he'd not been in the Saratoga winner's circle yet.

"Will we have something running in the big race this weekend?" they'd say and the Judge would bite his lip.

"Next week," he'd say and later he'd tell Ham they couldn't be running in claimers at Saratoga, they needed to win "something good."

Ham went along with it for the first two weeks when Lizzie made him skip a non-winners of two race he knew they could win and instead enter the grey filly Snowflake in the Schuylerville stakes and she finished dead last and the Judge left the track with a pout and didn't stop back at the barn afterwards. That was Ham's way of showing her what he'd been saying all along, that if they wanted to keep the Judge happy, putting him in the winners circle was the only way to do it.

The third week of the meet Ham found a maiden claimer to run their two year-old Raja Baba colt in, and he told Lizzie the colt was making some noise and his breathing wasn't good enough to get him far.

Lizzie said a few of their friends had been teasing the Judge and he didn't have much of a sense of humor when the ribbing was at his expense and when the colt won by ten the whole crew were delighted at having their picture taken, until the steward's assistant put the "CLAIMED" tag on its halter and the Judge's smile turned to a frown.

"Don't mind him," said Lizzie, "He's got too many advisors now."

But Lizzie, who should have known better, didn't come to Ham's defense and instead wore her guilty face in silence when the Judge made her come with him to the barn that evening while he sat Ham for a lecture.

"You've made me look like a fool," said the Judge, "Reggie says that horse could win the Derby next year and you just gave him away."

Ham was going to sit there and take it but instead he snapped.

"Your Honor, if that horse wins any Derby I'll eat him with a knife and fork. And any dope who tells you he will wouldn't know a racehorse from a goat," and he walked out the tack room door feeling unsure as to whether he'd still have a job in the morning.

Black Robe was in the mid-week feature, coming off a second place finish in a stake at Monmouth and Ham could feel the Judge's cold stare as he set the colt's saddle. They walked Black Robe under a tree and just as he was to give the rider a leg up, Lizzie whispered to Ham,

"Just stay out of his way, I'll handle him."

The horses were breaking from the post parade when Stella asked the Judge,

"Are you going to win?"

"We damn well better," said the Judge, the edge on his voice for Ham's benefit.

The track was still sloppy from a thunderstorm, but nobody cared about getting their shoes wet when they had to step out on the track to the chalk circle, even the Judge's friends in their expensive loafers, and a few clowned for the picture.

A reporter from the *Morning Telegraph* collared Lizzie and the Judge and Ham was just as happy to get away, following Black Robe and his groom to the test barn. By the time he got back, the Judge had departed but Lizzie was waiting in the tack room office.

"I'm sorry," she said, "We've not been getting along lately. It might get ugly."

"He likes to be right all the time," said Ham and she nodded agreement.

There were a couple of flattering articles in the *Morning Telegraph* and the *Saratogian* about Black Robe, saying maybe he'd be a candidate for the Travers and if not he'd be one to watch for the fall meet at Belmont.

All the stories told how the colt got his name, for the Judge's courtroom attire and given that by his loving wife

Elizabeth Barrett, who herself was named for her great-great aunt the famous poet although Ham knew that all to be a huge contrivance on Lizzie's part.

By Travers weekend Lizzie and the Judge had had it out more than a few times providing themselves as the source of ongoing entertainment for the racing public. At Villa Balsamo she threw a carafe of red wine that barely missed his head and the wall was still pink a week later.

At the Wishing Well they were asked to leave after Lizzie dumped succotash in the Judge's lap and the whole place saw him take a swing and a miss at her, but it served Lizzie's purpose and they were divorced in record time.

She said the Judge was a smart guy, but if he'd really been smart he would have had a pre-nup and he wouldn't have to give her all those millions, but such was the price of true love gone afoul.

Before she took off for a week at the Red Door, Lizzie bought Ham a new pickup truck and gave him a handful of cash and told him to pack up the outfit for Belmont, they'd be going back there to the old Evans' barn where it all started

Ham figured Spectacular Bid wouldn't run many more times, so when the crowd packed the place for the Woodward Stakes he parked himself in the spot where he and Willie used to hang out by the Belmont paddock. It had an odd feeling, watching only one horse circle the crowd inside the walking ring and a one-horse post parade.

But Spectacular Bid couldn't find any competition for his last start, having whipped them all year, so he got to go out in style with a "walkover," which meant he stood alone in the gate and was alone all the way around the track too.

When the fans exulted at their hero's performance Ham clapped right along with them as Buddy Delp and Willie Shoemaker saluted the throngs from the winner's circle and the owner held a bottle of Heineken aloft in his final toast.

CHAPTER 17

1981

Belmont became very quiet without the Judge and his chronic need for attention. Lizzie actually got on a few horses and galloped them and decided she had enough money to afford her keeping the stable until she figured out what else she wanted to do.

They had a dozen in the barn but most had turf pedigrees and it was a rainy fall so only a few got an opportunity to run when the races kept coming off the grass and by the end of the meet only two had made it to the winners circle.

It proved to be a good partnership between Ham and Lizzie, him doing the hands on work and her taking the accolades when they won. At Thanksgiving Ham took a week off and went to Vermont to see the family and when he got back Lizzie told him to pack the crew up and head to Hialeah. They got to Florida the week before Christmas and ended up in the small barn that sat behind the kitchen.

Whenever Ham walked with the horses down the pine-lined horse path from the barn and out across the parking lot to the quarter pole gap he thought of his time there with Willie and Mighty, how he and Willie had talked of maybe having a horse in the Kentucky Derby.

And it hadn't happened for them but he noticed how every January the trainers all asked each other who's your Derby horse and the old saw was if you didn't know by then you didn't have one.

Ham had Lizzie's barn running like a Swiss watch and Lizzie turned out to be a better promoter than anyone would have imagined, winning a few races and drinking Champagne in the Hialeah Turf Club every afternoon with Horatio Luro's crew.

She had a couple of older gentlemen who deluded themselves into believing they were as fascinating as she told them they were and she did a skillful job of separating the two when one or the other would show up every day at the track and buy her lunch.

Lizzie spent as much time as necessary on her hair and makeup and wore only Chanel to the races, and at thirty-two her youth put her on more or less even terms with the women in the Turf Club whose only advantage was their wealth. The few pounds she put on eating caviar and drinking Mimosas might have ended her career exercising horses but they looked good on her and she did the high life well.

And Lizzie was never short on attention when she came to the races, nor was she ever wanting for company when celebrating a trip to the winner's circle. An entourage developed quickly as she spread the Judge's alimony without restrain, and when she spared no expense to provide each of her horses with a shiny brass name-plate on their halter, Ham teased her that it was only because she couldn't figure out who was who.

The cadre she entertained were either widowed or divorced and Lizzie scandalized their female peers on a daily basis with a bawdy joke or lascivious gesture and she ran the Palm Beach crew's adrenaline as well as their testosterone to the limit when she displayed some cleavage and plenty of leg.

She managed to get those two suitors to compete for her attention by seeing how many horses they could stock her stable with, and by Groundhog Day she didn't have an empty stall in the barn.

It might have been just a coincidence that of all the horses those wealthy men bought and paid for, the ones that supported the stable and paid the feed bills and the vet bills, of all those horses the one that turned out best was the one that Lizzie owned all by herself.

After the three year old she had named The Earl broke his maiden by open lengths the first week at Hialeah, she set to extracting the maximum amount of attention she could drum up.

The press couldn't get enough of a pretty blonde divorcee who wore Hermes scarves and red lipstick, training what might turn out to be a Kentucky Derby horse, and she insisted on leading The Earl out to the walking ring rather than let them use flashbulbs in her barn.

She made a show of having the horse pick English candy from her pockets.

"He adores his Yorkie bars," she said,

"I have me mum post them from home. Otherwise he wants to be a bad boy."

There had only been three women ever to train a Kentucky Derby starter and Lizzie aimed to make everyone know she wasn't just going to Louisville for the mint juleps, she was out to win.

The Earl could be obstreperous and they all knew he'd once hurt a groom who didn't pay attention, cow-kicking him but he behaved like a pony when Lizzie took a hold of his shank.

And the vet said she should geld him but Lizzie said it would be too expensive a mistake when he won the Derby.

She trusted Ham and knew he was a better horseman, so she worked him like a borrowed mule, paying him well but insisting that he do all the hands-on work and he never balked, right there every time she batted her fake eyelashes at him.

The closest thing they had to a tense moment was one morning when a reporter ventured out past his depth when trying to play up her role as a woman in a male dominated world. He asked her if Ham was her only son and right after that Lizzie changed her style considerably, switching from expensive clothes to jeans and t-shirts and cowboy boots and a ball cap, but she still spent the time on her makeup and kept the red lipstick.

Ham walked The Earl into the paddock for his first stakes race and he had to put the saddle on and tighten the girth and even throw the rider up because the newspaper guys had Lizzie surrounded. She looked over and gave him a thumbs-up as if to say I'm busy and cover that for me will you.

It was a full field and The Earl wasn't one of the choices but when he moved to the lead turning for home the fans went wild.

Ham felt himself above the crowd, the garbled melee a couple of feet below him and he could see the jockey's lips moving but as he snapped the shank on the horse's bridle and led them into the winner's circle, words failed him.

The fans gathered five-deep at the fence as Lizzie threw kisses from the winners circle and as soon as he got back to the barn Ham put up some saw horses and went to the stable gate to ask Ted the security guard if he wanted to make some extra money, keeping folks out of their barn.

Ham remembered what it had been like having a Derby horse with J.B. and he figured the hordes would descend soon, looking for a piece of the best story in town.

"Who, me?" said Lizzie when reporters eager for anything resembling a story asked her if it was true she'd been in the movies back in England, not knowing she was the one who started the rumour.

Over the next few weeks the *Miami Herald*, the *Fort Lauderdale Sun-Sentinel* and the *New York Times* all ran feature stories on Lizzie, each with a different photo of her kissing her horse.

The Earl finished just out of the money in the Everglades stake but when she shipped him to New Orleans he won the prep there and it looked like a certainty he'd head for Churchill Downs until he started hacking his head off. Ham knew that was actually a good thing since besides the cough, he was getting a little ankle to boot.

"I hate the way people grind up a good horse just to be in the Derby," she said,

"We'll do the right thing and have a meal ticket for the rest of the year."

"No Derby for The Earl," Lizzie told the press, but when one of the old gents in the Turf Club asked her to go there with him, she promptly bought a hat and packed her bags for Louisville.

Lizzie came to the barn late one morning and gave Ham the checkbook again and told him to bring The Earl outside on the walking ring so she could say goodbye before he she left town.

The big bay hadn't been out of his stall for a couple of days, getting medicated and staying off that sore pastern, so when Ham went to fetch him he was more out of sorts than usual. Ham spoke softly to The Earl and wasn't paying that much attention as he used a soft brush and a rub-rag to dust him off and he didn't tie him to the back of the stall but let the colt stand free with his shank dangling. That's why he wasn't prepared the first time when the colt reared and as they exited the stall The Earl spun, slamming Ham into the wall. Ham crumpled like a rag-doll and slid to the ground.

Lizzie was waiting out at the ring and when she heard the commotion in the shedrow she yelled:

"Ham!"

And there was no answer but The Earl came trotting out of the barn with his shank trailing.

Lizzie felt under Ham's jaw for a pulse and ran to her office to punch 911 into the phone on her desk and called the stable office to alert security.

"It's Ham, he's breathing but he's not moving. Hurry," she said.

Hamilton Greer didn't get to see Pleasant Colony win the 1981 Wood Memorial or the Kentucky Derby or the Preakness.

And on Belmont day, it's more than likely he would have been rooting for the big bay and his rotund little Italian trainer to win the Triple Crown like everyone else in the racing world, but in June of '81 Hamilton was still lying unconcious in the semi-darkness of his room at Hialeah Hospital, getting help with his breathing from a machine.

Lizzie visited Ham every day for the first month or so until she sold The Earl and dispersed the other horses in her barn. She left a forwarding address and a phone number for her home in Kentucky and told Ham's doctor to call her if anything changed and when Jake came to visit Ham at the end of July, he was the first one other than Ham's mother that had come in nearly a month. Ham got his sustenance from a feeding tube and barely moved a twitch, even the times when he dreamed which was every day.

Ham's mother took a plane from Burlington the week it happened and came once a fortnight and stayed for a few days each time but when she flew down for his birthday in August she had pretty much resigned herself that he'd never come back to the world.

Ham dreamed he was walking with Willie through the crowd at Keeneland and everyone was looking at him and they were talking among themselves, pointing and shaking their heads and when he got to the winners circle he wasn't in it but hovering above, watching Willie and Lizzie and Hayley and Carla and the Judge and Mister Adams but it wasn't a horse the groom led in but a bear and he was startled but the rest just laughed.

Ham's mother was sitting in a straight-backed chair reading a *People* magazine when he spoke.

"I miss Willie," he said, and she jumped up and pushed the nurse-call button.

Summing beat Pleasant Colony in the Belmont but when the Derby winner went looking for revenge in the Travers, they both got dusted by Willow Hour and Ham wasn't there but he did watch the race on television from his hospital room.

The doctors said they had no explanation why he'd been out so long, just that he showed no sign of any long-term damage and if he did a couple of months of rehabilitation at the gym he should be okay to go on with his life.

Jake had a six-horse stable of cheap claimers at Calder that he was grinding out a living with and Ham started to go by early mornings and walk a few hots just to get back in the swing of things.

Ham didn't have a Florida driver's license but the track Chaplin vouched for him at the General Educational Development center and in a couple of months he managed to pass the test. He didn't tell his mom what he was doing but the first thing he did when he got the high school diploma in his hands was to mail it to her.

By the fall Ham was feeling pretty well and he rubbed three horses while Jake rubbed the other three and they hustled and won a race here and there.

They cashed one decent bet and even if they weren't prospering, they were surviving as they waited for a runner, for as Ham often liked say when he quoted Willie:

"A good horse can come from anywhere, 'might be right under your nose and you just have to be looking."

Ham picked up a sales catalog in the Ocala Breeders Sales office and asked the lady behind the counter for a pen before he headed out back to look at some of the two year olds.

"I remember you, didn't you train for that little guy from New Jersey," she said.

"Yes ma'am that was me," said Ham.

"You still got that cute wife that gallops?" she said, and Ham said no, that was a while ago and a lot of water's gone over the dam.

Ham was leaning on the rail watching the sales prospects as little chestnut filly caught his eye galloping by with her neck bowed, giving the girl riding her all she could handle, when he sensed someone standing close by.

It was Spider, but Ham did a double take, almost not sure it was the same guy he'd known. His face had lost some previously handsome features, a severe scar over his brow and the noble Roman nose was now a flattened beak reminiscent of a battered prize fighter from a fifties movie, but the rare smile was the same. And he'd aged more than a little since Ham's visit at Sing Sing.

"Hey," said Spider.

Ham's first reaction was to ask what happened to his face but instinct told him otherwise.

"Hey," he said, "You're back."

Then Ham asked him how long he'd been out of prison and if he was going to ride again, but he knew no track would give a jockey's license to someone with Spider's history.

Spider said the guys that got him in trouble in the first place had roughed him up and that was why he looked the way he did with the smushed up kisser.

301

"They wanted me to mule their coke and when I said 'no way' they used me for a punching bag, threw me in the trunk of a car. 'Guess I'm lucky I made it out alive," he said, better than his old man who'd died in prison.

Ham didn't know what else to say.

"At least you're around horses."

"Yeah," said Spider, "You don't need a license to ride at a farm."

They shot the breeze by the rail for a while and Ham thought to himself that the guy who had come out of prison wasn't the surly, sullen Spider he knew before.

He told Spider that he'd been away too, but not in the same way and he guessed it was taking both of them a little time to get back in the world.

"We each got kicked in different ways," said Spider.

"At least we're still here to tell about it," said Ham.

Spider gave Ham a business card that said "Horseman" with his address and phone and said maybe we can get together when you're in town, and no, I won't get in trouble again.

He said he was working on a farm with a trainer who'd gotten ruled off for cheating too, and laughed that they'd both learned their lesson the hard way.

"Birds of a feather..."

Ham and Jake liked to think they were lucky guys, hustling along and scraping out a living at the racetrack, a better place to be than a high-rise office building where they'd have to wear a tie and kowtow to a boss.

They'd bought and sold, bought and sold and made money and lost money and each of them were smart enough to have not run up any significant bills but in the end they were living on credit cards and soon they were falling behind again with the feed man and the blacksmith and the vet. But they both knew the horses they had wouldn't compete with the ones coming south in November, so they needed to make plans fast.

Jake wanted to try the Fair Grounds track in New Orleans for a while in hopes that new surroundings might change their luck. Ham agreed to that but didn't mention to Jake that he had it in the back of his mind maybe he'd see Molly if she and her father still ran their tack business there.

They packed up their tack and the Sallee van man gave them a bargain price to ship the horses if they didn't mind a lot of stops along the way. Ham sold his pickup truck and Jake managed to stuff all their personal possessions into his old VW Microbus and they left the same day the van pulled out, Sal Paradise and Dean Moriarty taking life as they found it.

Had they not gotten off the interstate to find some lunch outside Biloxi they wouldn't have been stopped at that intersection when the old lady in the Buick tail-ended them.

There wasn't any real damage to the VW and no doubt it was her fault, but Jake just said, "shit" and jumped back in and gunned the engine, cutting back to the highway and it was only about two or three miles before the trooper pulled them over for leaving the scene of an accident.

The next morning the jail-keeper unlocked the door to Ham's cell.

"You can hit the road," said the cop.

"What about Jake?" asked Ham.

"He's got an outstanding warrant for child support, the Feds are going to ship him back to Vermont," said the cop.

Ham left Biloxi with a few hundred in cash and the duffel bag he had hopped off the bus in Saratoga with almost a dozen years before and the cops weren't too bad, one of them giving him a ride to the bus station.

Before he got on the Greyhound he called the stable gate at Fair Grounds and told the guard what had happened and please ask someone to water off and feed those horses when they arrive and I'll be there as soon as I can.

CHAPTER 18

1982

For the first time in a decade Hamilton Greer found himself all alone. He was alone in the sense that other than his mother in Vermont, that he'd only been in touch with twice a year for the past ten years, everyone else was gone. There were plenty of people around, but none that he was close to. No one to ask when he had a question...

Willie was gone, Mister Evans was gone, Bogie and Jelly and Jake and all the women, Lizzie, Carla and Hayley, they were all gone too, some off to parts unknown and he'd lost touch with each of them.

As he threw the duffel bag over his shoulder Ham thanked the bus driver for dropping him only a block from the stable gate of the Fair Grounds racetrack.

The beige shirt of Leon Broussard's brown uniform was worn at the collar and his shirt tail was out, belying him more a homeless guy than a security guard, but he listened to Ham's story and took it at face value.

He joked to Ham that they were ready to put out a search warrant for him, since the horses had arrived in Jake's name and they'd been there in the barn relegated to transients and other scufflers eating charity feed for the past forty-eight hours.

"Hang in there, brother," said Leon, and he gave Ham a key to the tack room.

"But y'all be warned, Pauquette the stall man 'be around in the morning, looking for his pint of blood."

"Thanks," said Ham, clearly a beaten man at this point.

There were a few things missing from the pile of equipment, but fortunately the thieves hadn't taken all the pitchforks and rakes and the van guys had hung the cross ties and webbings and the horses each had their feed tubs and water buckets.

It wasn't until later that Ham realized the tack trunk with their exercise saddles and bridles had been emptied. But the thieves hadn't bothered with Ham's books or the cigar box with his letters from home and the rest of his clothes looked to be all there but when he realized the transistor radio was gone he just sat on the footlocker and let the wave of sorrow roll over him.

Ham took the horses out one at a time for a walk, first Jammy and then Fussball, then Melon Man and Dustbin and when he got the older geldings Bozzy and Kite Winder on the patch of grass for a graze, he apologized profusely to each for the lack of attention.

"Whatcha' get lost?" said an old woman whose horses occupied the neighboring stalls on that side of the barn.

Ham told her about Jake and the accident and no, he didn't know what he was going to do about the feed man, he'd try and figure that out soon, and yes, he would be rubbing all six of those horses himself.

"That's my straw they been sleeping on, you can parlay them a few more days," she said, meaning he could pick the manure out and not have to re-bed the stalls which wasn't a realistic option anyway.

"You been here before?" she said.

"No, ma'am," he said.

"Hope you got some cash," she said, "Nobody hereabouts gives credit to strangers," and Ham counted three hundred-sixty bucks left in his pocket after he gave her twenty for the straw and hay and oats.

When he asked her about Pauquette she said the man wore a black five-day shadow like Bluto in the Popeye cartoons and owed his job to being cousin to the track manager, otherwise he'd have been lucky to get the pearl diver's job in the track kitchen.

"Gimmie a hundred," said Pauquette, and Ham saw no way out but to pay since he needed the tack room to sleep in and couldn't afford to ship out if he wanted.

"I usually get twenty a stall," said Pauquette, implying that Ham should be grateful for the discount on his extortion.

After he went to the kitchen and ate his first meal in days Ham took two apples and a banana back to the barn and he was down to two hundred fifty and whatever change the Mason jar had in it.

Ham called the Sheriff's Office in Biloxi and left the number of the pay phone at the end of the barn, hoping he'd be close by if Jake got to call and later that afternoon he heard the ring.

"Bozzy okay?" said Jake, "Make sure you put that ointment in his eye."

"They're all a little skinny," said Ham.

"Looks like I'm going back to Vermont," said Jake, "and probably get and automatic six in the slammer. See if you can sell Jammy and Fussball and maybe you can hold on for a little. I'm really sorry, Ham."

Of the six, Jammy, Fussball and Melon Man had won their last starts, all for bottom claimers, but Dustbin, Bozzy and Kite Winder had nothing to recommend. At least Ham had the folder with their registration papers, so when the feed man came by he leaned on the awning and tried to be as up front as he could, offering a trade.

"If I took horses instead of money, I'd have been out of business a long time ago," said the feed man,

"I'll send Tee James over, he buys horses for Delta Downs, pays cash,"

"Tee" comes from the French word "petite" and is the what a lot of Cajuns call their kids instead of "junior" but Tee James wasn't petite at all, he looked like a Sumo wrestler with straight red hair that fringed his bald pate and swept back into the mullet that hung over his collar.

He bought Jammy on the spot for four thousand and told Ham he'd be back for Fussball with a guy who wanted to see him gallop and Ham said that was okay, he doesn't walk that great but he runs just fine.

When the tack truck rolled up, Ham was hoping it might be Molly, but her father said she'd quit the track, gone to Dallas to work in computers and good for her, 'cause this is a grind, selling hoof picks and halters to guys who can't pay.

Tee James and his man were there the next morning to check out Fussball and if the old gelding didn't wing his left front foot so wide when he galloped Ham could have gotten the four grand he was asking but it was easy for the buyer to sense his desperation so he had to settle for three. At least it let him pay for some feed and bedding and the used tack he bought from Holly's dad; two bridles, a set of reins and a saddle and a couple of halters better than the ones he had.

He signed the bill of sale and the foal papers as "agent" and took the other horses' papers to the racing office to give them to the Horse Identifier and he entered Melon Man and Bozzy in the cheapest races they ran there, beaten claimers for three thousand.

Melon Man finished a distant second and got claimed but Bozzy broke through the gate and ran off a half mile before the stewards ordered him scratched and when Ham got him back to the barn, his tendon reminded Ham of another of Willie's old expressions:

"Only one what likes a bow is Robin Hood."

At the end of the week he got another call from Jake to warn him that there was a lien coming from Vermont on anything that had his name on it.

"Sell everything before they get the letter," he said, but the stewards had already had a phone call from the state's attorney and a Sheriff came around with Pauquette and put a sign on the barn, saying that the horses and all the tack were going to be sold on the courthouse steps.

The Sheriff had a belly that hung over his belt and a Confederate flag sticker on the bumper of his car and he made a list of everything in the barn and told Ham and if he took anything they'd put his Yankee ass in jail for larceny.

Ham waited around until the deputies came to get the horses and paid off the feed man and Molly's father and the van bill and the blacksmith with the cash he had, leaving him with less than a thousand but still in possession of his good name.

Pauquette heard about the deal and came back to the barn and told Ham he needed a commission for sending Tee James around, which was of course not true and Ham hated to give the reprobate another fifty but he knew if he lost the tack room he'd have no where to sleep until he could find a job and the week before Christmas it wasn't likely anyone was hiring.

He made a few dollars walking hots in the mornings but the rest of the days Ham took to wandering the streets of New Orleans, parsing his dwindling assets and wondering how he'd survive.

But he sent the hundred-dollar bill to Vermont in a Christmas card even though it represented a substantial portion of his bankroll.

And he put on a good act on the phone at Christmas, telling his mom how great the oysters and the crawfish were and how he enjoyed a coffee au lait with a beignet every morning at the Café Du Monde. That wasn't far from the truth since there was no lack of help at the Fair Grounds track that winter and he couldn't even find a steady job walking hots and there was always a spot to sit and sip that bitter coffee.

In the winter of 1982 Mary Russ rode Lord Darnley in the Widener Stakes at Hialeah and became the first woman jockey to win a Grade I race, and a seven year old gelding named John Henry won the Santa Anita 'Big Cap.

But it wasn't a particularly notable crop of Kentucky Derby candidates and the winner turned out to be a grey colt named Gato del Sol who didn't win another race that year.

A week after the track closed for the season the kitchen closed and there were only a few stragglers left in the barn area and the stall man told them they'd all have to be gone in a few more days, 'cause he was turning off the water and electric and putting a padlock on the stable gate.

Hamilton Greer found himself in the soup line at the Ozanam Inn behind a man who said he'd been sleeping by the train tracks for a year. The guy said he'd been a teacher but his school had been forced to make cutbacks because of the recession and he'd been relegated to day work ever since. That had been just enough to pay for a rooming house until he couldn't find any work at all and gave up.

"I started on the racetrack about ten years ago and sometimes it was pretty good, until this year and everything fell apart for me too," said Ham.

Ham looked at the man's vacant eyes and wondered if his would become the same, full of uncertainty and disappointment and if that would happen to him, that he'd just pack it in and become another lost soul.

They took their gumbo to an empty table and spent the next half hour eating but neither could bring himself to say another word.

When he finished, Ham took his bowl and spoon to the counter and put them in the plastic bin with the other dirty dishes and when he looked back to the table the man was gone.

PART III

CHAPTER 19

1984

The day he had to leave the Fair Grounds barn area Ham stuffed all his possessions in his duffel bag and made his way to the Ozanam Inn. He'd been earning his meals there by doing chores and that was where he found himself, sleeping in a hostel-like dorm with a bunch of strangers.

Ham had few things left that he valued, not that he'd brought that much along as he moved about the country other than the cigar box and a few books. He sold the last of his books except a copy of Jensen's *Founding of a Nation* that Willie bequeathed which had notes in the margins in Willie's hand.

He left the black footlocker to the old lady at the barn, taking along just the clothes that fit and a leather dopp kit he'd also inherited from Willie that had been his brothers' from the First war. And for a moment he pondered hocking his grandfather's pocket watch, but reconsidered and decided he'd have to be starving to do that.

The Inn was filled with an eclectic mix of humanity; either men of the world who'd once won but eventually lost everything they had or those more simple souls whose penchant for the wanderlust compelled them to become creatures of the highway, attached to nothing.

Some drank to ease their spirit while others used whatever drug they thought might kill the pain, and many simply retreated into bitterness and detachment as a final resort. Ham began to find himself among the latter and avoided any interaction or conversation, rather cloistering himself in the extensive library at the shelter.

But the Brothers of St. Vincent de Paul who ran the refuge treated all who came there as equals and their motto was *"Give a fish today, teach to fish for tomorrow."*

Although he might have been from a different generation Brother Steven communicated well with the younger ones and wore the mantle of a sage. They talked about life and how each had arrived at the Inn, some as a result of a life filled with poor choices, most through no fault of their own, just the victims of bad luck.

"The solace we get from alcohol is as vacuous as the empty bottle it comes from. The thing about souls," said the Brother, "Everyone has one and sooner or later everyone bares it, either to another person or to God."

"I don't know what that means," said Ham.

Every morning at seven after he finished the communal breakfast Ham walked the mile and a half to the corner of South Maestri and St. Charles Streets by Lafayette Square and got in a queue with the others there, each hoping that someone might come along and summon them to a day's work for a day's pay.

One morning they'd be picking in the cotton fields and the next they'd be cutting sugar cane or digging up sweet potatoes or up a ladder in a tree picking pecans. Mostly it was dirty, heavy work, but Ham preferred that to hanging around the common area at the Inn, listening to the complainers blame everything else but themselves for their current state of misfortune.

After the sugar cane leaves left him bleeding, he decided that some sturdy gloves were going to be his best friends so he invested in a pair along with a straw hat with a wide brim.

And Ham reckoned that if you were clean-shaven and standing up straight, not slouching, you'd get picked first, so he found his razor and after Brother Andrew cut his hair he looked like a recruit at boot camp.

"Need one more for baling hay," yelled the boss in the Panama hat.

"I'm your man," said Ham, and he hopped in the back of a pickup truck with five other guys.

They worked until dusk, gathering the dry cut hay and hefting the finished sixty pound bales onto the back of flatbed trucks that would carry them to the feed yard.

"Want a couple 'week's work?" said the boss.

"I'm your man," said Ham.

"Artie's tractor trailer leaves Saturday morning for Hot Springs. Be at the park at five-thirty and he'll fetch y'all. You and him 'pick up the alfalfa 'over to Lafayette, head on up to Hot Springs. 'Hundred when you're done, sleep on the truck. Twenty of it up front but you 'paying for your own meals."

"Okay by me," said Ham and the man gave him two fives and a ten.

The cab of the tractor had a bunk behind the seats.

"It's okay if y'all want to catch some shut-eye back there," said Artie, "as long as you didn't mind me prattling on."

He was a little man but he had thick forearms and clutched the steering wheel with hands the size of ham hocks and he spit his chaw in a Styrofoam coffee cup and by the time they got to Lafayette he'd finished telling his life story.

Artie told Ham he'd grown up in Arkansas, second-last of six kids to a couple of factory workers and his mother had died after giving birth to the youngest and they were so dirt-poor that they could feel even the share croppers looking down on them.

"I heard Papa talking, how they were going to take me to Saint Joe's orphanage and give me up to them nuns, so I ran away, hid behind a bakery and survived off scraps," he said.

"How old?" said Ham.

"Twelve. 'Lived on the streets in Little Rock until I got 'sixteen, and then I lied about my age and joined up the army and got a free trip to France. Shot a bunch of them Nazis."

He told Ham they'd unload the bales of hay in the morning at the feed company's lot near the Oaklawn Park race track and reload the flatbed to turn right around with whatever the boss man had going back to New Orleans, probably from the depot in Little Rock. They'd never go back empty, even if it meant sleeping a night or two in the truck.

"One time I brung back a load of turkeys and they gobbled all the way. I liked that sound... kind of soothing, you know? I been making my wife get us a ham for Thanksgiving ever since then," he said.

By the time all the hay was loaded it was after ten when they got on the road. They rolled past Shreveport and up through Texarcana and by late afternoon they were making good time and the hills began to turn into mountains but Artie was still keeping his speed up like a man on a mission.

"You 'in for a treat, Yankee-boy," he said as they pulled into the blue stone parking lot of a barbecue joint with smoke pouring out of its chimney.

The crude painted sign at the roadside said Stubby's Hik'ry Pit and when they took their seats on a picnic bench Artie pointed to the menu on a chalkboard marked "Bar-B-Q Heaven."

The place was full of diners who had come there from the racetrack just down the road and winner's circle pictures dotted the walls. Ham wandered, looking for familiar faces and he found a couple of J.B.'s horses up there and got a bad taste in his mouth when he saw one of the photos with a gaunt Buster Brown surrounded by the dentist's gang after they won a cheap claimer.

It was near dark when they finished feasting on ribs and chicken and beer from a pitcher.

"On me, sonny," said Artie, and he waved at the waitress for his check and the waitress told him no it ain't Art-honey, it's on that guy over there.

"His horse won the big race today and he just picked up everybody's tab for the night," she said.

A white haired man with a little redhead and a tall guy with a handlebar moustache and a pretty blonde were leaving the restaurant to a hail of applause and some of the patrons stood and chanted:

"Wild-again, Wild-again, Wild-again..."

Ham kept at that job for about a month, riding shotgun for Artie and loading the trailer as they travelled back and forth to Arkansas. Each payday he threw a few dollars in the donation box at the Ozanam Inn and told the Brothers to pray for him.

Some days they drove hay or straw and other times they hauled heavy loads of concrete pipe or steel beams or shipping containers, chained tight to the flatbed.

"Think y'all can drive one of these rigs?" said Artie.

"Used to drive a twelve horse van, don't see why not," said Ham,

"You ever haul horses, Artie?"

"Not for me," said Artie, "They scare me... too damn big. I'm more a dog and cat man. Got two hounds and a tabby what thinks he's a dog too."

"You'd be okay with horses if you were around them a little," said Ham.

"Axe the boss man to give you a try, he needs him some drivers," said Artie.

Ham liked the feel of the open road as he shifted the gears of the tractor and let the eighteen-wheeler roll along on the broad stretches of country road, especially the smooth reddish-brown and pink highways of Arkansas.

The rig was over fifty feet long, and the tractor had twelve gears so for most of the trip when he got into high he didn't have to downshift unless he had to climb the hills between Little Rock and Hot Springs. The trailer was a flatbed just like Artie's and since most of the time he was hauling over fifty thousand pounds he needed the length of a football field to stop so he always gave himself plenty of room.

Ham began to think of that space behind the front seat as home and for the next couple of months he was on the road six days a week and when he wasn't driving he would grab a shower and have a rest in one of the dorm rooms at the truck depot. He started to scratch up a little bankroll and hid it up under the dash of the tractor behind the radio.

Woody Stephens trained a popular Derby winner for 1984 named Swale that was a son of the Triple Crown champion Seattle Slew but Woody's colt had folks scratching their heads when he threw in a clunker in the Preakness and finished seventh.

Plenty agreed with Woody that he was better than the rest of the three year-olds in his crop and might have been another Triple Crown horse if not for that off day in Baltimore, but the horse world was shocked when only a week after winning the Belmont, Swale dropped dead from what most supposed was a heart attack.

On Travers day in August of 1984 Ham was about fourteen hundred miles away from Saratoga, driving his rig from New Orleans to Little Rock, but he managed to time a mid-afternoon pit stop so he could pop into a country roadhouse and catch the race on television.

TV cameras panned across the track and the infield and the crowded grandstand and the boxes and that was all it took for his imagination to carry him right back there into the seats where he and Willie had watched Secretariat.

Without the Derby winner the race was pretty much void of importance, but Ham got a little rush and took to his feet as Carr de Naskra flashed a burst of speed at the wire to deny Pine Circle. He finished his Coke and hit the road.

"Watch yourself on this trip, son," said the boss man as the crew loaded containers onto Ham's flatbed.

"How's that?" said Ham.

"Union strike between here and Chicago."

"But we're not union," said Ham and the boss nodded.

"Exactly, they'll be looking for us" he said.

Ham made it to Bowling Green with a load for the new Walmart that had just opened there and after they unloaded his trailer he drove to the depot, prepared to sit there a day or two and wait for the boss to tell him where to go for his next pick-up. He was on a wooden bench outside the office reading a worn paperback of *On the Road* when the dispatcher called him to the phone.

"Get the hell out of there and head right back here pronto," said the boss.

"No pick-up?" said Ham.

"Just move," said the boss.

When Ham made the turn out of the industrial park, two cars blocked the road ahead and another two pulled up behind him, eliminating any chance of escape.

Four guys the size of gorillas went to work with baseball bats, smashing his grill and headlights and by the time they finished the side windows and the windshield, Ham was covered with bits of broken glass.

They hauled him out of the cab and didn't hit him in the face with their bats, just in his back and legs but their fists were hard enough to break his nose and as they drove off he spit out a tooth on the road and picked it up and put it in his pocket.

He lay there in the street for a while before he got enough strength to stagger back to the cab and when he went on the C.B radio looking for help, the two or three responders he did raise told him they hoped he and all the other scabs died out there on the road, so when he climbed down and sat on the curb he was glad to see the random driver not pass on by but pull over.

The doctor taped three broken ribs and bandaged his knee and head but he told Ham he was likely out of luck with his molar. He said that would need an implant, so Ham saved it in a small plastic bag just in case he was lucky enough to find a dentist that could make a match. They let him sleep on a gurney in the hallway so a nurse could check him overnight just in case he had a concussion and released him first thing the next morning.

When Ham called back to the office in New Orleans, the boss said they'd cover his expenses in the emergency room and could he maybe check on the tractor and let them know what it was going to take to get him back on the road.

Ham got a ride to the truck that morning and it was still in the street with yellow crime scene tape festooned about the cab. He figured he had nothing to lose so he climbed in and breathed a sigh of relief when he felt his packet of cash under the dash behind the radio. He shoved the money in his pocket and started the tractor and pulled the rig to the roadside, ripped off the rest of the tape and locked up the cab. He limped down the street and found a pay phone so he could call the boss.

"Just a lot of broken glass," he said.

"Get the windshield fixed and drive the tractor home, leave the flatbed there and they won't bother you," said the man.

"If it's all the same to you, I think I'd just as soon take off for a while," said Ham, "and give myself a chance to heal up."

After he finished paying for a couple of shirts and some jeans and a pair of shoes at Marshalls and buying a bus ticket, Ham counted a bit under two thousand dollars in his stash.

He left the keys to the truck at the depot and rode a Greyhound from Hot Springs that got him into Dallas in mid-afternoon. Before he got on the next bus to Tucson he asked for some directions and made the walk to Dealey Plaza to have a look at the place where President Kennedy had been shot.

Hamilton Greer had been seven years old and in the third grade when the Principal's voice came over the P.A. system and he recalled that day and how he and the other children had watched their teacher cry and how they'd cried too. He remembered how school ended early that day and how his mom and dad and he and his sisters gasped at the image of Jack Ruby shooting Lee Harvey Oswald right there on the little black and white TV in their living room and how no one got any sleep that night, already haunted by things they couldn't have imagined if they didn't see them with their own eyes.

Ham didn't know if he'd ever be in Dallas again, so that was his chance to see where it had happened; the street, the Book Depository from where they said Oswald had fired the lethal shots and the grassy knoll where some folks said other shots came from.

He thought it looked ordinary, a place where if you didn't know it was part of history, you'd walk right past, but he got a chill when he stood on the street by the spot where the President's blood had been spilled.

Ham walked back to the bus depot and bought a ticket from there to Tucson. A wiry little country-woman in the ticket line behind him gave him a tip as she dragged three squabbling brats behind her.

"Them Texas roads are rougher than the rock-pile on a Alabama chain gang," she said, "Git yourself some earplugs at the next stop if you expect to get any sleep."

Some think crossing Texas is like crossing an ocean. Most of it looks the same and it feels like you'll never see the end of rolling plains covered with sagebrush. Ham stared out the window at the miles of scrub until he put in the earplugs and fell asleep and the lady was right, he never heard the roar of those bus tires on the hard Lone Star roads.

Long journeys on public conveyances lend themselves to deep contemplation and on that one, staring at cacti and rocks and sagebrush for endless miles, Ham considered that he might try the desert life for a bit, but when he walked out onto the street at seven in the morning the thermometer at the Tucson bus depot read one-eleven and the air was so hot and dry he felt like he'd just swallowed a quart of dust.

He grabbed a Coke from a vending machine and jumped a local bus to the Tucson train station and spent the extra money for a ticket on the next Sunset Limited to Los Angeles.

An old Mexican lady was peddling tacos from a hand wagon and he ate half-a-dozen before she wrapped up a few in tinfoil for him to take along on the half-empty train. He found a pair of seats at the back of the last car and stretched out to watch the world go by until the sun went down.

The Limited gave him a twelve-hour look at an America nothing like anything he'd ever seen before, leaving the saguaro dotted Arizona desert as the train climbed the high desert of Palm Springs before it skirted the San Jacinto mountains and descended towards the coast.

For a guy who'd known nothing but mountains before his sixteenth birthday, he couldn't help but wonder at the vastness of the Pacific Ocean. He grabbed a few hours sleep but spent most of the trip with his gaze fixed on the space between him and the horizon.

Someone had abandoned a copy of the *Tucson Citizen* between the seats and when he turned to the sports page, horse racing was the cover story.

"Breeder's Cup," it said and Ham waxed nostalgic when he read stories about the new event, seven stakes races they would be putting on at Hollywood Park in three days. He read every word and started to imagine himself back at the paddock rail, watching the horses and their every move, just as he did at each of the tracks he'd inhabited for the past dozen years.

The sportswriters wrote about the odds and that made him think of Willie and some of the bets they'd made over the years and it was an involuntary motion when he touched the fold of bills in his pocket.

Horses always follow the money and the best of the best were showing up for purses that started at a million dollars, and Ham considered it might be the right time to be there and maybe he'd find some work with a good outfit, one with those top-class horses. If he felt really game, he might try to make some money gambling, seeing that he didn't have that much and maybe this was his time to get lucky. Like Willie said about the track:

"You can always come back."

It was turning dark when he shuffled through Union Station and Ham considered trying to spend the night there on a bench until he watched a cop roust another guy snoozing with his head on a duffel bag similar to his own.

He left the station and started walking aimlessly toward downtown Los Angeles until he came to a place where he realized the entire breadth of the sidewalk was populated by the homeless, sleeping on cardboard or right on the concrete or the few that had makeshift tents and no one cast an eye when he found a vacant doorway and curled up.

Ham's sleep that night was interrupted by fleeting dreams, as he felt himself floating high above the road while he watched his eighteen-wheeler ramble along below, following three grey horses that raced nose-and-nose, their tails trailing in the breeze. He saw himself in the cab of the tractor, shifting gears and accelerating off the top of a hill between two other tractor-trailers until those began to squeeze him, banging sides and shaking the steering wheel from his hands as he lost control.

When he awoke his hands were clenched, hard white balls of flesh and bone and sinew, and he was sweating.

Skid Row looked worse in the morning light. Ham passed through blocks of sidewalks crowded with cardboard lean-tos and a couple of times had to step over sleeping bodies swaddled in dirty blankets. He turned and headed back to the train station figuring he could hunker down for a few hours and when he closed his eyes to nap he clutched his used ticket on his chest like a ready traveler just in case any house cops should eyeball him.

The girl at the information booth told him there would be a bus to the track on Saturday morning, but he'd better be there early as it was a local and made a lot of stops. She told him about a flop in Chinatown that was only a few blocks' walk from the station and when he found the place it was over a restaurant and he gave twenty bucks up front for a room for two nights.

Ham slept in for the first day and on Friday he took a bus to Hollywood and walked the streets like a tourist and found James Dean's star and Marilyn Monroe's on the sidewalk, came back late and ate Chinese food and drank Chinese beer in the restaurant downstairs. He sat at a long communal table with a white tablecloth and before he knew it the place was full and he was the only one at the table with no Asian blood.

The girls giggled as he struggled with his chopsticks and one of the men asked him if he needed a fork but Ham determined not to let the tools defeat him and he was a good sport to provide the entertainment as he sprayed his rice all about. The girls coached him and before dinner was finished he had nearly mastered the utensils and they praised him in words he couldn't understand, but he got the idea.

On Saturday morning, Ham stashed his duffel bag in a locker at Union Station and he was first in line to board the bus to the track. He grabbed a seat near the driver in hopes he'd get a tour along the way if the guy were talkative. A little old lady asked if she could have the window seat.

"Who do you like in the first?" she said.

Ham hadn't picked up a *Racing Form* since he sold the last of Jake's horses in New Orleans so when she asked if he'd like to look at hers, he skimmed the card to see if he saw any familiar names. He didn't see many, but he saw plenty of familiar faces when half a dozen of the people from the Chinese restaurant got on the bus. Once again he had no idea what they were saying but smiled back.

And the bus wasn't a local but it wasn't exactly an express either. They stopped three times and each time the people who climbed on were dressed up, men in suits and ties and the women with hats that matched their dresses and all buzzing about the horses they were off to see, the best ones they'd ever see.

The driver pointed out the Hollywood sign on a distant hill and the huge donut on the roof of Randy's, but otherwise Ham could tell the guy was too concerned about what he was going to wager on, asking every other passenger "who ya like?" as they got on the bus.

"I think this horse "Eillo" will win the sprint," said the old lady,

"His name is Ollie spelled backwards. My late husband was named Ollie. He was a nice man."

"As good a way as any, sometimes," said Ham.

Ham still had his laminated license from New York and when he flashed it at the pass gate he kept his thumb over the date and the guard just glanced at the picture and waved him past into Hollywood Park. Ham figured he might as well push his luck and stuck out his left hand for the guy to stamp with invisible ink, marking him so he could cross into the clubhouse.

"Thanks," said Ham and the guard gave him a program.

"Thanks again," said Ham.

Ham hadn't been around a crowded racetrack for quite a while, let alone one with sixty thousand fans but that was what they had at Hollywood Park in 1984. He wandered the gardens by the Native Diver statue and went out front to the paddock to watch the horses enter for each race and after the Paddock Judge would call "riders up" he made his way to the fence just so he could get as close as possible to the track and hear the thunder of hoofbeats when they drove to the finish line.

He made a halfhearted bet in the first race and of course it lost.

Ham laughed to himself when Eillo won the sprint, thinking maybe that was what he should do, bet on horses that strangers gave him or keep his money in his pocket.

Other than the two eastern horses, Eillo and the two-year old colt Chief's Crown, Ham wasn't familiar with the rest of the horses. Europeans took the turf events and west coast trainers and jockeys seemed to be dominating on their home court, but Ham felt himself being drawn back into their world.

He was at the front of the building standing in line to get a hot dog at the grill near the paddock walking ring, when he realized the white haired man in front of him looked familiar. He had on the same black blazer he wore in Hot Springs but now he had a white moustache that matched his hair.

The guy started to reach into his pocket to pay for his burger when Ham grabbed the opportunity to return a favor.

"On me," said Ham, " I owe you one from the Hik'ry Pit back on Oaklawn Handicap day when you paid for the house. It's good luck to do the right thing."

"Gol Dang," said the man, "If that ain't nice of you, son. And I'll take all the good luck I can get."

"You're in the big one," said Ham.

"He's going to win and you can bet anything you want on that, son," said the man and he gave Ham a wink before he disappeared into the crowd.

Ham hung by the paddock while the two-year olds circled and a couple of the eastern horses caught his eye, Spend A Buck and Chief's Crown.

He made a twenty dollar exacta box with the two and bet fifty on Spend A Buck to win and at the eighth pole it looked like he might cash both tickets until Chief's Crown drew off to win and Tank's Prospect edged Spend A Buck out for second in the last few jumps.

After he ripped up his losing tickets he went back to his spot at the paddock and waited for the horses to come out for the big race, the Classic. No one had ever run for a three million dollar purse before and he wanted to see if those horses looked any different than the ones he'd been rubbing and running for a lot, lot less money.

Gate Dancer was a monster and looked even bigger with the earmuffs Van Berg came up with to keep him from coming unglued at the crowd sounds. Slew o' Gold was just as big and they looked the best two on the walking ring. Wild Again passed in front of Ham and he reckoned the little black horse was almost a head shorter than the other two but he never discounted any horse on size, remembering Willie's words:

"It ain't the size of the dog in the fight, it's the fight in the dog what matters." And when Ham said yeah but horses aren't dogs, Willie had smiled and said no they ain't but they do have to fight if they're going to win.

As the horses approached the gate for the big race, Ham peeked up at the odds board and saw thirty-to-one on Wild Again and when he looked in the paddock he saw the man with the white-hair laughing.

More of Willie's words rung in his ears:

"If you're gonna make a bet on a longshot, make it count. Nobody ever changed anything in their life betting two bucks on a favorite."

Ham counted every cent he had left and it came to twenty bucks short of sixteen hundred dollars. He peeled off a thousand and shoved the rest back in his jeans, headed for the seller and put five hundred to win and five hundred to place on number two, Wild Again, and stuck the tickets in his shirt pocket.

EPILOGUE

Wild Again had to survive an inquiry and claims of foul from Gate Dancer and Slew 'o Gold before he got to become the official winner of the first Breeder's Cup Classic.

There was no doubt that considerable bumping went on through the stretch and although he was a head shorter in size to the other two Wild Again didn't come up short on heart. When he stuck his nose in front at the wire Pat Day pointed to heaven in thanks to the Lord and that was the way the stewards saw it too, leaving him up as the winner.

Hamilton Greer took just over thirty thousand dollars from the cashier's window at Hollywood Park on that Breeder's Cup afternoon, pitched the cashier a hundred and rode a yellow cab back to Union Station.

He told the driver to wait while he retrieved his duffel bag from the locker and had the man drop him off on a corner in Westwood where he walked the streets until he found a small rooming house with a vacancy sign and checked in. The following morning he found a newsstand and bought a *New York Times*, a *Los Angeles Times* and a *Daily Racing Form* and spent the rest of the day reading in a small park while he considered his future. Hamilton Greer decided it was time to settle down and here was as good a place as any to start putting down those roots Willie spoke about, plus, his luck at the windows brought just enough cash to change his perspective.

Monday morning he took a bus to Santa Monica and took a number at the DMV to turn in his Vermont driver's license for a California one. He stopped at the first bank he saw and opened a bank account to keep his new-found capital safe and walked the length of Wilshire Boulevard back home to his lodging just so he could get familiar with the area.

On Saturday morning Ham took a pre-dawn cab ride back to Hollywood Park and paced the stable area from end to end. He ran into a few horsemen he'd known from Belmont and Saratoga and one of them, a trainer named Bobby Frankel, said he remembered him and Willie when they worked for J.B.

"We used to call you 'the Odd Couple,'" said Frankel.

He told Ham that it was a surprise to him that J.B. turned out to be a cheating low-life.